MEDICINE MAN

Memoir of a Cancer Physician

Peter Kennedy MD

© 2015 Peter Kennedy MD
All rights reserved.

ISBN-13: 978-1512196603
ISBN-10: 1512196606

CHAPTER ONE

I snapped awake as the overhead paging system called my name. I had dozed off while writing a progress note at the nursing station. I'd had no sleep for three days, except for a couple of hours Friday night as the medicine resident on call in the Yale–New Haven Hospital ER. It was Monday. The wall clock said seven fifteen. My shift was over. My head was clogged with a stuffy, marshmallowy feeling. My legs and back felt heavy as lead. They burned and ached and protested with each step I took. I trudged through the shock room. It had been cleaned after the last gunshot wound of the night had been taken to the OR. There were a couple of tired, runny-nosed kids in urgent care, whining, restless, and clinging to their mothers. They'd been there for a couple of hours. Dr. Tim O'Rourke could see them— he was going into pediatrics anyway.

The far end of the parking lot was dark as pitch. The cold wind off the Atlantic caught in my throat like a shard of glass. It was painful to take a breath. Crusted snowdrifts from a storm the week before blocked my path. I was too exhausted to climb them, too numbed to navigate around. My only thoughts were of Anne and our two squirmy daughters, who would be gleeful that I was home. I struggled across the parking lot to my car, a $200 cast-off Nash Rambler I'd bought for my daily three-and-a-half-mile hospital commute. In my head I was falling to the floor with Martha and Sara in not-so-mock exhaustion. Following my melodramatic collapse, I was usually too tired to stand again. The kids and Anne made a ritual of getting me on my feet. The girls would giggle and poke me with their little fists as I dozed at the dinner table. Imagining us at home helped revive my fatigue-fogged brain.

As a second-year resident in medicine at the Yale–New Haven Hospital, my fatigue was compounded by recent confrontations with demanding, pedantic professors who proclaimed that patient care was to be performed "the Yale way." My fellow residents were incredibly bright and capable, but many were trapped behind what I perceived as an Ivy League wall of blind acceptance. In my experience, few ever considered trying to figure out how to get over or around it.

I was ill fitted to that philosophy. I took pride in doing what I knew was needed to make a diagnosis, to respond quickly to a medical emergency, or to simply find the quickest way to get critically important information. It seemed I was always bumping heads with famous Yale physicians who were critical of my approach. At Baylor College of Medicine, where I'd trained as a medical student, aggressiveness and action had been nurtured and encouraged. And I'd loved every minute of it, graduating with highest honors and with a graduate degree to boot.

But not here.

Early on in my ER rotation, I had been called to the carpet because I had placed a large-bore tube (subclavian catheter) into the vein that passed beneath the collarbone of a tiny old lady who was so dehydrated that all her peripheral veins were completely collapsed. She was unresponsive, and she was bone dry. She had to have IV fluids. I had felt that placing a subclavian catheter was the most efficient way to get fluids into her. I had inserted the catheter and had fluids running in a few moments.

The next day, after morning report, where physicians reviewed the shift's activities and pending problems with house staff arriving for the following day, I was called to meet with the chief resident and the medicine department chair, an internationally heralded kidney specialist. I was surprised. And unnerved. What had I done now?

"Placing that line was too risky! You might have collapsed a lung."

The chief resident then informed me that the "old woman" had been Betty Finch Smith!

I had no idea who she was.

"She wrote *A Tree Grows in Brooklyn*. If she had died from a complication of our treatment, the press coverage could have been uncomfortable. You must be alert for things like that. How is she now?"

"Her numbers are better. She's making urine again. And she's awake. But she's confused and uncommunicative, which is her baseline. She was a nursing home transfer. No family listed. Somebody there felt like she was too dry. They don't like patients to die in those facilities. It's bad for their statistics."

"What was the serum sodium level?"

"One hundred seventy-seven. Could be a world's record!"

"Well, have a care. In the future, do a cutdown, or call the surgeons for a line. We don't like subclavian catheters here at Yale because of the very real potential for complications—bleeding, collapsed lung, infection, and such. By the way, have you placed many subclavian lines where you were trained?"

"About a hundred and twenty."

"That's quite a few. Any major complications?"

"Infection is always a risk in some patients. As a complication of the procedure itself—no. But every now and then I simply can't get into the vein."

Nobody said anything further. I guessed I'd been excused. But I was not convinced their admonition had been valid. In one sense I was a rebel. I knew what I knew: I'd used the means at hand, and it had worked on the poor old author, as I'd done with over a hundred patients in the past. It was a matter of facing a problem with the tools at hand and fixing it as fast and efficiently as I could.

Twenty-four hours later, Ms. Smith's blood sodium was returning to normal, and her dehydration was resolved. And she was still a senile little old lady being shipped back to her nursing home.

Two weeks later, some of the surgical residents came to me as a group. They wanted to learn how to place subclavian catheters. I was delighted! We held secret clinics where I instructed them on the tricks I'd learned about performing the procedure safely.

At the end of my first year at Yale, my residency class had presented me with a bloodstained harpoon, a comic tribute to my aggressiveness.

Now, as I labored through the parking lot still clad in OR greens and a wrinkled, body fluid–stained lab coat, two orderlies ran past me pushing a gurney.

One shouted, "She got shot! Some guy shot a tech in the vivarium!"

I turned slowly, swore quietly, and followed them. I knew the general surgical house staff was still in the OR. Who was available to handle the shock room? It was up to me again, despite my fatigue.

The orderlies transferred the woman to the exam table in the main shock room. Nurses began to cut her clothes off. I got a brief glimpse of a name tag—Mim…something. Then the clothes were in a pile in the corner. Glancing quickly at the woman, I could see she'd been shot once above the left nipple. She was unconscious, unresponsive. And she was getting bluer by the second.

"Get a line into her," I shouted.

As nurses and the ER intern examined her arms and feet, I grabbed a subclavian catheter from my private stash in a top drawer, splashed some antiseptic on her chest, and slid the line into place. I didn't bother with local anesthetic—she was not feeling anything. I secured the catheter with a couple of hastily placed skin sutures. The process took about a minute.

"Goddamn Ivy League baloney!" I thought to myself. "This lady needs a hose—*now!*"

The ER staff quickly rolled her onto her side so I could check for other signs of trauma, including the bullet's exit wound. There were none.

I was in an automatic mode now, repeating lifesaving exercises in medical emergencies I'd observed and performed many times before. There was no time to ponder, to weigh alternatives or options. I was on familiar ground. My fatigue vanished.

"Normal saline! Wide open!" I demanded. "Try to get a peripheral line into her. I need all the usual labs. Set her up for five units of blood, stat. Use the femoral vein to get samples if you have to! Get a foley catheter into her bladder. Send her urine to the lab-- if she's making any. Has she got a pulse?"

"Feeble," said the ER head nurse. The EKG leads were on her chest now, showing regular electrical heart activity.

"Tilt the head of the table down! Tube her! Bag her!" The anesthesiologist on call had left his OR, and had quietly entered the shock room. He slipped an endotracheal tube quickly into place from her mouth downward and into her trachea.

"I *love* you guys!" I cried. "You're always there *exactly* when I need you!"

He checked each side of her chest for breath sounds. "Nothing on the left side, but it's not due to my tube." He slipped out the door to return to his operating room duties. A respiratory therapist was now in the room, squeezing a rubber Ambu bag to force air into her lungs.

The absence of audible breath sounds on the left indicated that something was between the chest wall and the lung. In the setting of an acute traumatic wound to the left chest, it was either air--or, more likely, blood.

"We need a surgeon, right *now*!" Thoughts of sleep, dinner, my young daughters, and Anne vanished as if they never had existed. "We need a chest surgeon, *stat*!"

"Pulse?"

"Can't feel it!" This from a nurse who could find a pulse in a tree branch.

"Pump her! External massage." I was yelling again, with excitement and fear. This woman was dying! I needed surgical help! No familiar, calm face entered the room to aid my efforts or to support my decisions.

I splashed some brown antiseptic on her left chest. "Get me a chest tube tray, stat." The ER head nurse had it at the ready. She'd seen more of this stuff than I ever would. I made an inch-long incision below the patient's armpit in the space between her fifth and sixth rib, and felt a "pop" as I entered the space between the pleura—the satiny covering of the lung—which adhered to the chest wall and to the lung itself.

There was little or no drainage, and no "h-s-s-s-s" of exiting air, which would signify trapped air from the gunshot wound compressing the lung.

"Shit! That's gotta be all clot. We can't get drainage. Hook the tube to suction and water seal. Now!"

I heard someone say, "No pulse with chest compression!" We were all scared now. Where was the damn surgeon? We had to circulate her blood, or she would surely die.

I called out loudly, "Get me a thoracic tray. I need to do open massage on her."

I didn't lift my gaze to meet that of the ER charge nurse. If she didn't approve, I didn't want to know it. There wasn't time to waste on decorum or protocol. I splashed more iodine solution on her chest.

"Let's go, people. I need you all with me, or this lady's gonna die!"

By this time two units of unmatched, type-specific blood were hanging and flowing into her veins under pressure. She'd received more than three liters of IV saline, and still there was no pulse. Her heart was making a regular electrical rhythm, but the heart muscle wasn't pumping blood. All that saline, and most of her own four liters of blood, was in her chest cavity!

The single remaining heroic, potentially life-saving option was to pump the heart by hand. To get at it in an emergency setting involved cutting through the ribs on both sides of the breastbone and lifting the front of the chest and the breastbone up like a book cover.

I was a medical resident acting like a surgeon! I was out of my domain! But I had to do something. Her life was ebbing away before my eyes!

There was no time for a full surgical prep. She was a goner if oxygen didn't get to her brain immediately! I used an electric saw to transect the ribs from below her armpits to the bottom of her ribcage, first on the right and then on the left. Then using an electric cutting knife (Bovie), which coagulated tissue and vessels as it cut, I transected the tissues across the bottom of her ribs below the sternum. I cut the diaphragm from its moorings along the ribs and stuck my hand inside the pericardium, the fibrous sack encasing the heart. The heart was too small. Its chambers were getting no blood. I felt inside the left chest cavity. It was a swamp of clots.

"Lift her ribs up so I can *see* something!"

I felt desperately for the hole I knew had to be in the pulmonary artery, the largest vessel supplying blood from the right heart to the lung. But I couldn't find landmarks in the soup of clots and blood that filled her left chest.

In my gut, I knew I'd crossed the line from brash to brazen. I wasn't going to save this woman's life. My gloved hands were floating in my own sweat, despite the cool temperature in the shock room. I lost precious seconds as I felt for the torn pulmonary artery. I had to clamp it, or all the volume we poured into her would simply rush out the hole the bullet had made.

Suddenly, I felt a presence just behind me. It was Craig Meyers, the third-year chest-surgery resident. He reached around my arm and placed a large clamp across the left main pulmonary artery. He had not even needed a landmark to "fish" by.

"Jesus Christ!" Craig murmured to me. "The shooter couldn't have picked a better spot if he drew a target on her chest."

"Thank God! I'm glad you're here! Pressure? Any pulse?" I called out as I rhythmically squeezed the heart. "Craig, is there anything left to do I haven't done?"

"Nada, Doc."

I continued to squeeze her heart. I'd taken this whole team of nurses, therapists, techs, and physicians so far to prevent this lady's death. I couldn't quit now, standing in the middle of the carnage I'd caused. I squeezed rhythmically. What the hell was I going to do now?

Moments passed. Each one seemed like forever.

Then I heard, "She's fixed, Dr. Kennedy." The charge nurse had checked the patient's pupils. They were dilated and showed no change in size when a bright light was passed in front of them. Her brain had been without blood flow for too long. She was dead.

"EKG?"

I already knew the answer. The heart was a bag of wriggling worms in my hand—the last desperate throes of a dying heart.

"V-tach! No! It's V-fib," the tech monitoring the EKG called out. There was no effective electrical activity to drive the heart as a pump.

I was suddenly as exhausted as I had been when I crossed the parking lot less than thirty minutes ago.

It was over.

I was out of bright ideas or aggressive maneuvers.

Why had I tried so hard? To what purpose had I cut this poor woman up like a side of beef? This was not just an extra mile. This had been a whole new race. A sense of panic suddenly made it hard to breathe.

"Craig, am I going to get eaten alive by the surgical profs for this? I'm thinking back on all that stuff about the subclavian lines."

"I wouldn't worry. You did just fine. I'm sorry I didn't get here earlier. Not the prettiest operation I've ever seen. But you got where you needed to go. You made the right call. I'll clear it up with the faculty attending staff. When the chart comes through Medical Records, make sure it goes into my box. And call me to remind me, just to be sure."

I thanked the ER team members for their help and covered the woman's body with a sheet. I walked slowly to the corner of the shock room. I found myself sifting through the woman's discarded clothes. I found her employee's plastic name tag. "Means," I read. "Sandy Means."

I gasped as if I'd been shot.

"I know this name!"

Sandy had been a classmate of mine in medical school at Baylor. She had been in an MD/PhD program with me in Houston. I hadn't known her, except on sight. But I had known her aunt, Noreen Means, a superb pediatric surgeon. She had given lectures to my med school class. I had even observed her in the operating room. Somehow, I recalled that Sandy and Dr. Means had been very close.

I was too tired to think, to be properly deferential. But how could I *not* contact her? What would I say? Could I answer her questions? What would she say in response to what I had done to her niece?

I picked up a phone in the doctors' lounge. I felt miserable, physically spent, and inadequate, but I reminded myself that Sandy's decisions, and their consequences—whatever they had been—were hers, not mine. Whatever her story was, I had done my best to keep her alive at its end.

I found Dr. Means' number through the operator at MD Anderson Hospital.

"Dr. Means, this is Dr. Peter Kennedy, calling you from the Yale–New Haven Hospital. I was a student at Baylor; I spent a little time with you in a surgery rotation.

"Dr. Means, I'm so sorry. I'm calling with awful news. Your niece, Sandy, is dead. She was shot by some fellow who trapped her in the animal lab here at Yale...That's right.

He shot her in the chest at close range. Then he killed himself…I know. She was in the rat lab. No, I don't know why or how long she'd been here. This is my second year here, and I'd never seen her…Uh, I know nothing about details of their…We did everything we could, but he got her in the pulmonary artery, near the main trunk…That's right, the PA. We tried all the stuff we knew and some I had to make up. Everybody here was super. We really pushed the envelope for her…Yes, I was in the combined degree program with her. I'm so very sorry for your loss."

The words sounded empty, hollow. I was already agonizing over my inability to clamp the left pulmonary artery. I kept seeing her chest cavity, filled with blood and clots. The surgery resident had found it in a second! My God! I cut her up like a calf, and then I couldn't do what I needed to do.

Dr. Means was silent for a long moment. I heard only her quiet breathing. She said, "I know you did what you could." Then there was nothing.

I never saw or heard from her again, although I returned to Houston—and to Baylor—the following year.

Over the next twelve hours, the details of Sandy's life and death filtered in, mostly through the hospital staff. Sandy had left Baylor for Laos in 1969; she never finished her studies. She was protesting the war. She met and married a Laotian man so that he could gain entry to the United States. After returning to America, she tried to distance herself from the fellow. She took several tech-level positions as she worked her way across the country. Finally, she wound up in New Haven and essentially hid out in the animal lab, cleaning cages and feeding rats. But he still stalked her, found her there, cornered her, shot her at close range, and then killed himself with a round to his head.

Images of Sandy Means's body on the shock room table kept flashing through my head like foul, harassing nightmares. I kept seeing her left chest, full of blood, clots, and collapsed lung. I kept reliving my futile efforts to compress her heart, small and empty of blood. Did I do enough? Fast enough? Well enough?

Whatever. I'd done it.

Sandy Means would haunt me for years to come. I had been in a struggle for my life, for all my life. But pride, persistence, cockiness, competence, commitment, success, and bravado could not fill the void I felt this night. The pain of my seconds of indecision and my failure in that desperate situation would slip away slowly as life moved on: My parents died. Anne somehow stuck by me despite my passionate commitment to my patients and my career. My children thrived, grew, and later married. And I became comfortable with my profession choice of cancer care.

But the death of Sandy Means would remain in that dark place where options had run out, where even prayer left me facing a blind end, a cold, stone wall where I was alone, afraid, helpless, and in charge of something I could not control and that would never end.

CHAPTER TWO

John Augustus Kennedy stood on the foredeck of the *Marie Picard*, a tramp steamer that ferried emigrants from Liverpool, England, to Montreal, province of Quebec, Canada. He shook a pudgy fist at the fog enveloping him and the ship that would bear him, his wife, and his son, Leo, across the Atlantic to a new life in North America. His voice quivered with poorly controlled rage,

"Mary, Mother of God, I have waited too long, and planned too goddamn much, to allow this voyage to be delayed by a little *mist!*" His coarse tweed greatcoat flapped uselessly about his short legs. He was quite drunk and had slept little the night before. The send-off he had received from his friends and cronies on the Liverpool docks had begun several days before.

John Augustus, or Jack, as he was known, had worked around the docks since he was ten years old. He had been a stevedore, a blacksmith, and a small-time numbers runner. He was a strutting, cocky young man of short stature.

In time, he learned to use the normal tricks of the dock to pad his income. But the increasingly close scrutiny by Liverpool's port authority made it prudent that he relocate his family to Canada in 1912. Although he was a man with little formal education, Jack had carefully planned and saved enough to enable him to open a small ship hostelry soon after his arrival in Montreal.

Jack was married to his childhood sweetheart, Lillian Bullen. They were an item from the day they met. He was five, and she was four years old. Their parents were next-door neighbors in the Little Ireland section of Liverpool.

Lillian's father was a generous, loquacious man with a great handlebar beer-stained moustache. He drove a team of black Percherons on the docks by day and drank and sang in the local pubs by night. Jack's father, however, had been an inconsistent provider and a drunkard. His exploits later became explicitly absent from the family lore. His wife had left him to an unknown fate. A working mother, she was only occasionally present during Jack's waking hours. Because the children were clearly inseparable, the Bullen family took over much of the task of raising young Jack.

In time, Jack and Lillian married. She bore him three children, John Leo, George Thomas, and Lillian. The elder Lillian's life was not easy. There was generally enough money to pay for food and shelter, but she was too often the object of her husband's wrath. In her later years, when I saw her, Lillian was a woefully thin woman who spasmodically blinked and constantly swiveled her head like a sparrow. Some said she was "strange." But she had cared for her children and supported her husband as best she could. There were many young men like Jack in Little Ireland, and family abuse was commonplace. She did what she knew to do, and endured. When Jack died at age eighty-three, his wife joined him within three weeks.

Jack Kennedy was quick to rage, especially when he had been drinking, which was nightly. His habit was to return home after the family had eaten their dinner. His children were wise and quick enough to head for parts unknown when he trudged loudly up the steps to their second-story flat, howling curses at the injustices—real and imagined—of the day. But Lillian was a step slower and knew in her heart that Jack was a good man. She bore the brunt of much verbal and physical abuse. The kitchen was the most frequent battlefield. At such times, kitchen chairs, windows, and even the kitchen table were fair game for Jack's excesses.

The Kennedy clan had a fascination with violence and firearms, perhaps a consequence of its long history as mercenaries in Ireland. Jack was an avid hunter. He relished the relaxation and camaraderie that a hunting expedition provided, perhaps more than he loved the wild forests of Quebec. It was said he was a crack shot with both handgun and rifle.

But as he aged, Jack's immense strength turned to fat—he was just over five feet tall and weighed 240 pounds. He was still hugely powerful through his arms and chest, but adventures in the forest became increasingly difficult. His last hunting expedition was cut short because Jack burst his appendix while deep in the Laurentian Mountains. His comrades had to carry him off the mountain on a door.

Jack demanded that his sons should dedicate themselves to his business in the hostelry. But each son had very different ambitions. George longed to be a musician. Leo was determined to be a writer. The younger son remained with his father. He would die of alcoholism at a young age. His brother, John Leo, doggedly pursued his dream. And he was to achieve considerable success. Nevertheless, Leo would carry his hatred for his father like a wielded ax.

Little Leo Kennedy, as he was known on his block, had been sickly as a young boy. He was diagnosed with tuberculosis and sent to his grandmother's house to take the "cure" in England. When he returned to Montreal, his father's tantrums were in full, fiery bloom.

Young Leo was a bookish sort. He never learned to throw or catch a ball. He ran with his fingers spread before him like tongs of a rake. He bore the brunt of endless heckling and taunts by his schoolmates. Despite his father's insistence that he learn to box, Leo was a timid pugilist, a skill almost compulsory for a slightly built boy in a Catholic public school.

Leo quit school after the sixth grade to assist his father in the family business as a bookkeeper. He would not enter a middle or high school for over forty years.

Leo found both refuge and fascination in books. He knew the whereabouts of every used bookstore in Montreal and was never seen without an armload of written treasures to explore. At age ten he was writing book reviews and an occasional column in the Montreal English-language newspaper under a nom de plume.

When he was twelve years old, Leo was determined to protect his mother from his father's rages. When Jack Kennedy returned home in his usual state, Leo met him with an air rifle at the ready. He calmly announced that he would kill Jack if he hit Lillian again. Jack fell silent, his head bowed, his thick shoulders drooped. He gently took the gun from his son, sat at the newly repaired kitchen table, and sobbed.

Soon thereafter, Leo escaped his father's influence, and his expectations, by signing on as a cabin boy on a ship bound for the West Indies. He waited the officers' mess, cleaned their quarters, and washed and pressed their clothes. He returned home after three years with a head full of dreams and wild adventures.

He proudly presented his parents with a saki monkey as a welcome home gift. The monkey was quickly dispatched after it showed a predilection for climbing Lillian's white lace kitchen curtains with muddy feet and throwing his scat at his hosts with unerring accuracy.

By the time he was sixteen, Leo was absolutely certain that he was not suited for a life at sea or his father's business. He was going to become a writer.

Leo knew Montreal, and he knew where the books were. Through his bookstore contacts, he sought out fledgling authors like himself at bookshops and bars. McGill University was a stone's throw away from the family home and was a gathering place for young artists, writers, and thinkers. In general, these young men were college students, and came from affluent families. Leo was the youngest, and by far the least accomplished with regard to formal schooling. But his wit and his way with words made him readily accepted. The group held court in the Kennedy attic. Huddled around the chimney, which provided warmth against the bitter cold of Montreal in winter, the little band shared ideas and shouted loud approval of clever phrases and images.

As the young men gained experience and confidence, their mission was to defy the aging, "establishment" Canadian Victorian poets and essayists. The little group was convinced that their elder counterparts clung to a Victorian vestige in their writings. Collectively, the rebels published an assertive, out-front collection of essays and poems of their own. It was called the *Dial*, and it openly scorned the Canadian literati of the day.

When talk of war became widespread, Leo volunteered to fight Franco in Spain, like many writers of the time. But a rare, harmless disorder of sugar excretion in the urine (pentosuria) made his urine test appear as if he had diabetes. He was turned away from any active duty.

He saw and immediately loved a willowy Jewish girl. They married and had a son, Stephen. Miriam had full-time employment, but Leo's contribution as a starving writer was woefully small. Ironically, his wife was more upset that he traveled to Chicago and New York in search of work as a writer.

In the early 1930s Leo had a book of verse published by Macmillan & Co. He was being paid for his book reviews and essays. He was highly regarded in Canada's literary circles. McGill University granted him an equivalency diploma, based largely on his knowledge of post-Elizabethan literature, his published essays, and his verse.

But he was poor as dirt. He needed money to support his family.

Eventually, he and Miriam divorced. She remained in Canada to raise their son. Leo took his word craft skills to Detroit in search of a job in advertising. While seeking interviews for ad work, he chanced upon an open meeting of the local Communist Party. He spied a slightly built young Jewish woman who looked to him like Nefertiti in the flesh. She had enormous dark eyes and a lovely, open smile. But she had a sharp, agile tongue. She argued with revolutionaries and Bolsheviks with equal fury. Leo was breathless at her beauty. He was deaf to speeches and retorts. His mouth was dry as stone. He could not speak. His heart raced and threatened to burst from his chest. Her name was Esther.

He pursued her. She, in turn, was taken with his established position as a writer and his old-world attentiveness and charm. As a second-generation immigrant from a Jewish ghetto in Latvia, working as a secretary, she found him quite enchanting.

They were married in 1940.

I was born in 1944. Survival was to be my most immediate challenge.

CHAPTER THREE

I was born a strapping three-and-a-half-pound preemie. In the mid-1940s, babies like me almost always died. So it was my good fortune to be born in Chicago, where the first premature infant care unit in the country had been recently established. I am convinced that stroke of circumstance gave me a leg up on my survival. Actually, my father had moved his wife to the Windy City before he knew about me. He was learning a new trade, paying his dues, and struggling up his ladder of achievement in the advertising business. It was pure luck for me.

I was a sick little kid with multiple congenital disorders, a few of which demanded immediate attention. I had an inguinal hernia: for a year I wore a truss made from a sugar spoon. My left eye was permanently misaligned. More ominously, I had blockage of my ureters, the tubes that carry urine from the kidneys to the bladder. During my first three and a half years, doctors operated on my abdomen six times, moving my intestines aside in order to fashion a functioning, permanent drainage system for my kidneys. A final emergency operation through my left flank was required to completely remove my left kidney, which had become seriously infected.

Somewhere amid all those operations, illness, and hospital stays, I had my first mind-popping, forever-loving memory. I looked through bars in a dimly lit room at a woman with a gleaming, luminous white dress and white hat. I hurt badly in my belly when I tried to move, but I was compelled to sit up. I smelled the intoxicating scent of grape juice. (I now know that I was in a postoperative care setting, with a nurse sitting in my room—and I was about to be given my first post-op taste of liquid.)

My second memory was just as compelling. Someone had taken me to the shore of Lake Michigan. It was bitterly cold. The wind was so strong it blew my father off his feet. I hated it—my belly and my side hurt badly. My face felt like a frigid stone. I was carried into a dark, warm room filled floor to ceiling with golden tiles. And the smell was wonderful! It was smoky and slightly metallic. It was everywhere. It coated my face, my tongue. I was sure it would enter the fabric of my jacket so I could carry it home with me. Then it was explained to me. I was in a smokehouse, staring at racks of golden smoked whitefish.

That was it. That was my first four years.

Over the years, my mother assured me repeatedly that she fought like a tiger to keep me alive during those crises. The doctors gave up on me time after time.

"He cannot survive all this," they told her.

Of course, I was in no position to argue pro or con. I was either at home throwing up from kidney failure or in the hospital getting sliced open again. (There were no readily available blood tests to measure kidney damage in children at the time.) As I grew older, I felt my mother had used up all the tiger in her and had nothing left to give. There were times when I was deeply ambivalent that I had survived at all. I was to learn much later the issues with my mother were far more complex than I could have known.

When I was five, we moved from Chicago to South Norwalk, Connecticut. My father was an up-and-coming advertising copywriter, and he was drawn to the Mecca for copywriters, New York City. My concerns were somewhat more immediate. In 1948, our house was altered forever by the arrival of my younger sister, Deborah, or Debbie. From the day she first came home, it seemed she hated me. She yelled and bucked and stiffened at my mere presence.

My mother said, "She just has to get used to you, Peter."

That day, for reasons far beyond my control, would never come.

My first real memory of an *event* was Hurricane Carol, which devastated the Atlantic seaboard in 1954. It destroyed half the city of Norwalk. I accompanied my father and two of his friends while he checked on the status of his heavy wooden rowboat, which was docked at a place called Rowayton. The wind's force was terrifying. The swirling wind blew salty, icy water in my face and hid in wait for me around every corner, doorway, and alley. There was no place to hide from it.

Our companions, an older man and his blond-haired wife (I had never seen such yellow hair!), checked their much-larger boat moored next to ours. The woman grabbed the gunwale of her craft just as it collided with its neighbor. She shrieked and then fell. I watched in helpless terror as the two men fought the wind and the wild rocking of the boats to free her. Her fingers were twisted in wildly impossible directions. She would not look at them. She was strangely calm as she lay on the dock, despite the howling wind and cold. (I would have been screaming bloody murder!) Her husband gave her something from a small, flat silver container, which she drank eagerly.

The men half carried, half dragged her away from the boats to shore. I followed behind as best I could, grabbing at each stanchion as I inched my way to the parking lot. I was frantic with terror. I was convinced that I, too, was going to be crushed between the wildly bucking craft along the pier.

After Hurricane Carol, we moved again to a new house in Norwalk. The house had a huge backyard. It was a forest of oak trees, which stretched as far as I could run and ended abruptly atop a cliff. At the bottom was a pile of felled trees and then more forest. In the autumn, my father would rake leaves into a massive, soft pile of sweet smells, scratchy stems, and rustling noises—it was marvelous to leap onto its cushion, to become lost in its dim, dappled light.

It was in Norwalk that I first went to elementary school and made my first friend. An orange bus picked us up in the morning and brought us home at night. I loved school. I knew the answers to all the questions asked of us, and the teachers liked me, and they spoke in friendly tones to me.

Recess was another thing altogether. I was a lonely little kid who had not a clue how to play with other children. As winter brought snow and ice and cold winds, I stood in a corner of the playground and wept in dismay and hopelessness. How could I fit in? I couldn't throw or catch a ball. My efforts at kickball were humiliating. I was the last to be chosen for every game or event. And I was freezing!

I briefly contemplated putting my tongue on the jungle gym just to gain attention. (I'd seen it done. It worked! But getting unstuck from a freezing metal bar was bloody work. I simply lacked the courage.) My only reprieve was the end-of-recess bell. I could get warm and be liked by someone—even a teacher—for a time, anyway.

I had one friend, Joey Rezone. He was even smaller and less assertive than I was. His family lived at the top of a steep hill, which began its upward slope immediately beside our house. He'd learned to fight from his big brother and was eager to beat up any kid who challenged him—or me. He wore scuffed, worn-out shoes with huge holes in the soles. The cuffs of his pants were ragged from dragging in the street. He could run faster than the wind, his short little legs a blur as he fairly flew over the pavement. Joey spoke English badly. I thought it was due to his bad teeth. He never spoke up in class. When called upon, he'd laugh and squirm in his chair and say nothing. I hurt for his embarrassment.

Joey's father, Tony, was a taxi driver in Norwalk. He spoke little English and shouted curses in Italian from his porch atop the hill.. I never saw the objects of his rage. Whoever it was, I was frightened enough for both of us. I heard a startling blast from Tony's shotgun only once while we were neighbors. I was grateful that the Rezones were our friends. How could we survive if they were our enemies?

Often Tony would invite my father, with me in tow, to his house for spaghetti and rabbit. His wife prepared a massive bowl of spaghetti with red sauce, and Tony would dispatch one of the rabbits or a chicken he raised in pens in his backyard. Mrs. Rezone was a short, thick woman who spoke little and rarely smiled. When she did speak, I couldn't understand her. Both she and her husband had somehow lost most of their teeth, which made an eerie, jack-o'-lantern sight when they laughed. On occasion my father and I would trudge up the hill to sit with the Rezones on their porch. They drank from a large clay jug. After a few drinks from the jug, Joey got to have a turn too. I learned Mr. Rezone and his wife had come from Italy. They were always dirty and smelled bad. Joey and his mom smelled like old spaghetti sauce.

On one afternoon, the Rezone's oldest son, Tommy, took Joey and me to their fort in back of their house. There, he mounted his sister, doggie style, and they moved back and forth while they looked up at us and laughed. I had no idea what they were doing, and the not knowing made me feel uncomfortable.

My mother never participated in these weekend neighborhood outings. I figured she was taking care of Debbie. They were apparently never invited.

When I began school, my mother's sleep pattern was a deep mystery to me. She slept till past noon every day, and then stayed up reading the newspaper until long after we were put to bed. She read the paper all day and all night long, it seemed.

I learned early on that she *was not* available to make my breakfast. My father enjoyed the task heartily, but he fed us kids curried beef kidneys, stewed squirrel, or other critters he had killed in the backyard. Debbie loved such fare, but I did not! As an alternative, I learned to heat a slice of bologna in a small pan, place it on a piece of bread, and slather it with mustard. Not a feast, but it would do. We were never offered oatmeal or cold cereal and milk, like the other kids. I didn't know that Rice Krispies existed!

I always felt strangely disquieted by my choice of a morning meal. Then during the last weeks of first grade, the ax fell. We were told to write down what we'd had for breakfast and hand it in! Miss Gunderson, our teacher, read them aloud. I was mortified! My worst nightmare was about to come true. I would be more an outcast than ever. She got through Malt-O-Meal, scrambled eggs, Cheerios, and toast with jam without a hitch. Then she hesitated: "Bologn…er…bread…er…" Her voice lowered to a whisper. "Mustard."

What was I to do? I had never considered lying, by far an easier alternative. That did it. Life was over! Again. A week later, a nurse from the school came to our house to discuss nutrition with my mother. My mom never mentioned it to me. In fact, my father told the story to his friends one evening after the visit. Their barking laughter only shamed me more.

And my mother still read the newspaper and slept till noon.

Second grade was worse than first grade because most of the kids were bigger and stronger. In desperation, I tried Joey's technique of fighting for acceptance. My classmates were always teasing me, and my usual response was tears or running away. On one occasion I fought back. I took a wild swing and hit my tormenter in the mouth. I was immediately impressed at how soft his mouth was. But the kid collapsed, howling as if the hounds of hell were upon him. I wound up in the principal's office, a rarity for me, and escaped with a brief rebuke and a warning.

But the shame and pain I felt after my violent outburst made me feel awful. I never told my parents. I got no satisfaction from my lucky punch. It was not the answer for me.

Still, I craved attention, or at least recognition from the school kids. Perhaps if I could make them laugh…

I had an inspiration. I began drawing blackboard pictures of "Martians' brains" during show and tell. People laughed…and wanted more. I was a clown!

I was ecstatic! It beat fighting, and it surely beat crying in the corner of the schoolyard. The playground heckling continued, but it was less caustic. I became a performer at the daily show-and-tell sessions. The girls began to tease me, but it was gentle play. I was in heaven!

One unforgettable night, I was wakened by my sister's sobs and by loud noises. It was not another hurricane. There was yelling and sounds of things breaking coming from my parents' bedroom across the hall. I was scared enough, but Debbie was hysterical. I pulled her into the coat closet, and we sat, knees drawn under our chins, afraid to move or speak, for the rest of the night. My father found us. He seemed none the worse for wear. But I caught a glimpse of my mother in her darkened bedroom weeping softly as we passed. No one ever spoke of that night or of what we had witnessed.

Soon after, my father announced we were moving to Minnesota. I was despondent and confused. Just when my young life was looking up. Was it related to the sounds in the bedroom? Was that my fault? There were no answers for decades. We piled into our 1952 Plymouth and headed west.

We passed through unfamiliar country for days. We spent each night in dingy motels that smelled like moldy rags and cigarettes. My sister complained, wailed, wept, scratched, and screamed. She enforced "her side of the seat" line with fiery, violent resolve.

We began to see license plates marked "Land of 10,000 Lakes". At last we began to see...not blue water but endless cornfields and flat, flat countryside. At the point when my sister and I were preparing ourselves for mutual destruction, we stopped in front of a white house with peppermint awnings and a large fenced-in yard. And ten feet beyond the fence was a lake. The water was called Lake Minnetonka. It was blue as the sky! It was to be the setting where I found new skills and tasted independence, achievement, and heartbreaking emptiness over the next decade.

CHAPTER FOUR

Just like that, I became a Minnesota kid. During our first autumn as residents in the tiny hamlet of Tonka Bay (population 1,500 souls), I explored my turf and learned how to throw and hit a baseball, taught by the neighborhood kids. I was grateful that my new friends were more forgiving of my deficiencies and insecurities than my previous schoolmates had been.

We were a mixed bag. There were two boys older than me by three or four years. The eldest, Johnny, would one day become an off-Broadway costume designer, while Fred became an engineer. Johnny's younger brother, Darrel, was known as The Wolf. The slightest insult or injury induced howling, which could be heard all over the neighborhood. Our next-door neighbor's daughter, Susan, was a tomboy, the first and only I'd ever known. Although she was a few months younger than I, her daring-do as a swimmer, skater, and wielder of the baseball bat were a source of my envy and fascination.

We played baseball in our front yard after school when the light was good. A wire fence surrounded both the front and back yards—which made parents more comfortable than if we'd played in the street, although traffic was sparse on Lakeview Drive. During the summer, we crafted exotic model houses with French windows, vast staircases, and ballrooms out of balsa wood, fabric, and cardboard. By Thanksgiving, every year, the ice in front of the house was thick enough to skate on. Solid ice began about three feet beyond our fence, and because it usually hadn't snowed much by late November, the ice was a sheet of glass that swept on forever.

My new home had two stories, with an attic above and an enormous basement below. That basement was my father's *sanctum santorum*. As large as the perimeter of the house itself, it was lined with countless books stacked floor to ceiling and packed into every conceivable corner. An old metal desk had been wedged against one wall. Upon it sat a single fluorescent light shaped like a halo that reminded me of a snake in a storybook that ate its own tail. A much-used Royal typewriter sat in the center of its circle of light. My father sat under that harsh white halo, hunched over his writing machine, clacking away. He used only the middle finger of each hand to punch the keys, but the clack of the keys sounded like a machine-gun burst, followed by *scr-r-r-i-t-ch* and a *thwack* as he reloaded for another volley of clacks.

On the main floor was a glass-walled porch, which in summer served no purpose I could see. But in winter it was a linoleum hockey rink, a great place for stick handling and maneuvering a tennis ball instead of a hard rubber puck. As I grew more proficient, I paid too often to repair broken windows caused by shots gone astray. In addition, my indoor rink became a massive deep freeze where my mother stored her stews and casseroles so they could be enjoyed again and again…and again.

Our backyard was the neighborhood center for congregating kids. Sitting in the far portion of the yard, just before it sloped to the fence and the tiny beach beyond, was an enormous, gnarled birch tree. It was not one of the graceful stately birches one sees in pictures. It was bigger around than two grown men could reach. At a height of six feet, one limb turned at a right angle over the fence and the water beyond, while the rest of the tree fanned up and out to form a large shady area.

It was stalwart, and except for the weight it bore after winter snows and the coming and going of leaves with the seasons, it was unchanging. Its bark was silvery white but with great black scars and rough horny patches that chafed your legs when you shinnied out on its branches. The delicate scars of names with hearts and arrows through them were concentrated near its base, forgotten commitments of eternal or summer-long infatuations scratched with a nail or a knife blade, never to be erased.

We played cowboys in its branches, urging our birch limb on and up to conquer imaginary foes, and we challenged each other to see who could climb highest and farthest away from that indomitable trunk.

When we were older, we dropped to the water below, which had its own perils. At that rather shallow depth, the sand was often covered by slimy lake weed, which was slippery and coated your feet and legs with nasty green stuff. And one had to be alert to avoid hitting a swimmer or an incoming motorboat. Our beach was a busy place in the summer, and the birch tree was witness to it all.

Two matronly, full-bodied spaniels, one a springer spaniel and the other a cocker (both named Cookie), waded in the shallows from dawn till dinner chasing the tiny minnows that favored the shorefront. Their tails, cut to nubs as puppies, wagged constantly like some kind of independent propulsion system as they herded schools of tiny fish back and forth along the beachfront. At day's end, they closed up shop and returned home to be fed anything but minnows. Both dogs were hugely fat and remained so despite their daily travails.

Every July 4 my friends and I staked out a branch on the old birch to gaze at the fireworks we could see soaring over the Excelsior Amusement Park, about a mile and a half away as the boat sails. Before and after the show, we would fashion our own silent, magical fireworks in a bottle made from hostage fireflies.

The fireflies had to compete with mosquitoes that were abundant around the old birch. Before traipsing to the lake, we were slathered with bug repellent by our mothers --we all stank of diluted kerosene. But I was silently proud. It was *my* beach that was chosen as a playground and neighborhood swimming area.

July slipped into the dog days of August. Algae began to choke the shallow portions of the bay. On warm, clear mornings when the surface of the lake was as smooth as glass, I watched in fascination from my overhanging birch station as seemingly endless migrations of bluegills, crappies, bass, northern pike, and even walleyes passed unhurriedly beneath my birch. There was nothing to do but watch. These fish were not interested in eating worms, flies, or lures. Nothing could divert them from their appointed task. I never knew if they returned in the cooler evening or if this procession happened every day. But by September they bit and fought my lures as valiantly as ever.

Once or twice a year the loon drifted past our dock, a long-necked water bird that lived and nested with its mate at the shallow, swamp-like corner of Gideon's bay. It appeared only on gray overcast mornings in springtime and in late summer, when mist and fog covered much of the bay. Its presence was announced by a loud, long, laughing sound (from which the loon got its name). Alerted by its call, I raced out to our dock and peered through the mist to catch sight of the bird itself. I only actually saw it once or twice. Most of my "sightings" were merely "hearings".

The air, and the water below, cools quickly in Minnesota. The birch was an early warning system for us. Its leaves turned bright yellow early in the fall. It was time to grumble and rake up the leaves from birch, maple, and oak. But by the week before Thanksgiving, without fail, the bay froze over and transported kids on skates or using skate sails at dizzying speeds out of Gideon's Bay, around the point and onward to the Narrows Bridge, which seemed miles away.

In late November, there was little snow, and a kid on skates could deke and swerve like Henri Richard around defensemen and hit tremendous, rising slap shots past the goalie's outstretched arm. (Of course, at a dollar a puck, one had to chase and retrieve it.) The feeling of being able to skate on glass-smooth ice forever offered an exhilarating taste of freedom. Tired, cold, and hungry, I returned home at dusk. My landmark was always the giant hanging limb, standing black and twisted against the darkening sky.

When school began, we were bused to a consolidated grade school located in the little town of Excelsior. When we reached seventh grade, we joined with yet another passel of strangers as two more districts were merged. Finally, we were merged again as we became the business end of Minnetonka high school. The significance was that as playmates, competitors, and achievers, we had to adapt to a whole new population of students every two or three years, kids who already had predictable, stable associations and an established pecking order. The school system provided opportunity for fluidity and movement among its students. That would be an important part of my growth.

But upon my arrival to Lake Minnetonka, that meant nothing to me. I rode the bus to school every day, a bright kid, anxious to please. But I was finally growing strong enough from swimming, ice skating, and running that I could hold my own against my mates. I was no longer the last, reluctantly chosen one in the games we played. Sometimes, I was the choos*er*.

At home, my gang of five was still the center of my world. A favorite outing was a trip by skates or galoshes to Big Island, a sizable island in the middle of the lake, which had been home to an amusement park in the 1950s. We explored the ruins of the place itself or made a cooking fire in the ice and delighted in the roastables we stole from our various pantries.

One event during those early years on Lake Minnetonka stood in stark contrast to the usual business of growing up. I enjoyed exploring my parents' closets. I loved the smells, the hidden corners, and the mysteries they contained. During one such morning adventure, I came upon a massive glass jar filled with white capsules. I staggered out to the foot of my mother's bed, my head and trunk partially hidden by this huge new treasure.

"Hey. What's this?" I cried, laughing.

The mother who couldn't move to make breakfast leaped from her bed like a tiger defending her cubs.

Only I wasn't the object of any protective instinct.

She was protecting the jar! Her face contorted with rage, she grabbed a belt and set the jar safely aside. She didn't say a word. Then she struck at me repeatedly with the belt, using both the leather and the buckle end. It was the only physical beating she ever gave me. I was frightened more by her rage and her focused intensity than I was hurt by the beating. I had never seen my mother behave like this before. And I had no idea what I'd done.

I never forgot her look, her never-seen-before efficiency of movement, or her ferocity. But it would be decades before I understood what lay behind it.

My father's presence was a magical event during those early years. He had left for work long before I wakened each morning. He arrived home late at night; I delighted in his man smell, the scratchiness of his greatcoat and his whiskers, the sweetish smell of his breath.

He never ate his meals with us. When the lake was not covered with ice, he took rod and reel to the end of our dock to catch bluegills, bass, or the occasional bullhead, a small catfish. He cooked them himself, poured some bad-smelling liquid into a large aluminum glass, and retired to his cave. Down the stairs, I could hear his typewriter clacking away as he ate and drank and wrote. Often, we could hear Elizabethan music played *loud*. Soon thereafter, Shakespeare's plays replaced the lute and the flute. Even gentle tunes at that volume made my mother's china rattle.

On weekends, Leo was engaged in self-appointed tasks long before I got up, the ubiquitous aluminum glass never far away. He usually napped in the late afternoon or fished with his friends from the ad agency. After his dinner, he often told my mother how much he loved her. And she looked up from her crossword puzzle and said nothing.

One hot summer afternoon, a friend and I were keeping cool by spraying each other with garden hoses. I ran into our garage for cover, and my chum sprayed my father's workbench and some of his tools. I was running for cover again, when someone tripped me from behind. I fell nose first on the concrete floor. I rolled onto my back only to see a length of chain falling from somewhere above me. Once. Again. Again. I was startled, frightened, confused. My father's arm was at the end of the chain. My playmate had long since run for safety.

My first thought was, "*Who is* this guy?"

The face above me was fiery red, contorted with rage. There was no sound except for his loud snorts of breath and the *clank* and *thunk* of the chain landing on concrete—and on my chest. No expression of outrage, no sound from Leo at all. Seconds later (although it seemed like forever) he abruptly turned away from me and entered his library.

That was the only time he ever struck me, but he did it with such a vengeance! I never really understood why it had happened. All that anger over a few wet tools? He would have been better served by making us dry and buff each and every "damaged" piece of equipment. I stayed far from him for several weeks, especially on weekends.

Our house was fifty feet from Gideon's Bay, which measured roughly three-quarters of a mile across and a mile and a half in length. At the closed end of the bay, to the west, tall reeds, lily pads, and cattails abounded. Redwing blackbirds were drawn by the lure of small fish and insects, all plentiful in the shallows. Outboard motor propellers fouled in the dense vegetation, and boats grounded themselves on submerged islands. It was not a place for boaters or water skiers. This was Leo's favorite fishing spot. Large-mouthed bass, northern pike, and the occasional walleyed pike were taken with spinning tackle and lightweight monofilament line. Bluegills, perch, and the occasional crappie waited for fishermen just beyond the limits of our boat dock. But to take a big bass deep in the local wilderness was another adventure altogether.

At its southeast end, the bay opened into an even larger area that featured the town of Excelsior. Like most of Minnesota's ten thousand lakes, Minnetonka's borders had been formed as glaciers from another age retreated north. Most of the state's glacial lakes had myriads of inlets and small bays, the nooks and crannies left by the massive ice sheets. Our lake was no exception. Small islands were scattered about the lake, remnants of land somehow spared by the retreating glacier. They were ripe for exploration by preteen children. The largest of these, suitably called Big Island, was perfect for campouts. The ruins of an old amusement park were stark testimony to the local inhabitants' fruitless efforts to attract paying visitors.

By age twelve, I was allowed to explore the lake's glorious mysteries in our fourteen-foot aluminum rowboat. The craft was powered by a pokey ten-horsepower outboard motor. But speed was not my issue then. It was freedom! Freedom from whatever it was that made me feel like someone was running fingernails down a blackboard—constantly!

I could reach virtually any corner of my known world by boat. I rejoiced at my independence. I flat out loved it.

I began to spend more time with new friends my age, and I met and enjoyed their parents. Almost immediately, one observation shocked me like an ice bath. These adults behaved like an entirely different species from my own parents. A casual expression of affection, a sarcastic remark expressed with love rather than anger, a touch on the arm, and a quick hug were sensations that I hadn't known before. Unconsciously, I began to reorder my life so I could observe and experience more of those strange but wonderful feelings. Sleepovers were common, even on school nights, and I slept away nearly as often as I slept at home.

My boat became a sacred vehicle. I found I could take it within hailing distance of the local municipal golf course. I had caddied at the course previously. I was paid fifty cents to carry a golf bag over eighteen holes. The best jobs were on Sunday morning. If I carried two bags, I got a dollar! Now I had access to freedom and to *spending power!*

The following spring the club manager, a man named Rusty, approached me. He was a tall, gravelly voiced fellow,, thin across the chest and shoulders, and bulbous through the waist. He offered me a steady job working after school and weekends cleaning the members' golf clubs and straightening the pro shop. I was so excited, I asked if I could begin that very day!

Because I was in or around the pro shop every day, I got to meet and interact with the club members. They spoke to me; some made jokes at my expense. More than occasionally, they actually recognized I was there. Best of all, now I had money for gasoline, golf balls, and even a few used golf clubs. I learned the game of golf, hitting golf balls into the lake from my back yard, or on the course's practice, tee. I hit golf balls whenever I had free time, often until it was too dark to see their flight. Then I trudged the half mile to my boat. Since my rowboat had no running lights for safety and visibility, I used a flashlight to mark my presence and direction during the fifteen-minute trip across Gideon's bay to the house with the peppermint awnings.

My parents never seemed interested in my new "career." My father offered no objection, and my mother still slept till noon and read the newspaper until long after we had gone to bed each night.

Academic achievement at my consolidated junior high school was not a big deal. It just sort of happened. I took a standardized examination while in seventh grade. My teachers made much ado about the fact that I ranked with high school seniors in mathematics, and they mentioned something about college level in English something or other. I brought the news home to my family. No one raised an eyebrow.

By age thirteen, a certain wildness, a frequent passion to create adventure out of daily life, became supremely important. And the Narrows Bridge provided perfect adventure-seeking opportunities. It spanned the canal that connected the upper and lower portions of Lake Minnetonka. It was fifty feet high. Friends and I reconnoitered near the bridge. We reveled not just over the jump but in measuring how close we could come to boats passing beneath the bridge. We never considered injury, or death, or the fact that we put the fear of God into more than one unsuspecting boater as he and his party got a brief glimpse of a squealing body in tennis shoes and swim trunks fall from the sky.

During winters, we learned to drive old automobiles on frozen Lake Minnetonka. My first drive was in a 1935 black Buick, which Leo had bought to haul his icehouse—a canvas sheet draped over a flimsy frame but adequate cover for a day, or a night, spent ice fishing. Each year, a couple of our classmates (and an unknown number of visitors to the lake) would get too drunk or too daring and venture over parts of the lake where the ice was too thin to bear the considerable weight of an automobile. Each year, Minnetonka residents mourned the loss of one or two of their own to the frigid waters of the lake. We local folks knew where the areas were and steered clear of them.

My crew didn't lack for relatively safer thrills, including skate sailing—we rigged a sheet to a pole as long as two broomsticks and held it into the wind while on ice skates. The speed was exhilarating. The danger was the presence of huge cracks in the ice that could trap a skate and stop one's momentum instantly. The consequences of such an event often included a broken ankle, sprained knee, or a fractured leg.

Iceboats were the zenith of excitement and luxury on frozen Lake Minnetonka. They boasted seats of sorts, extra warm coats, scarves, and gloves, plus room for sodas or food. Their sails were huge, designed to catch the icy winds blowing across the lake. And those craft could fairly *fly*. They often raced in packs on Minnetonka ice.

Speed on the lake—frozen or not—was a sign of adolescent daring. I needed more speed for my rowboat. I had found an old wooden fourteen-foot runabout with a large outboard engine, priced for quick sale. Runabout was a fancy name for a rowboat with a deck across its bow and a wheel to steer instead of a stick. The wheel was far superior to the stick in terms of status. I diverted my golf earnings into the boat, only to realize its back end, or transom, was rotted and leaked more water than I could bail or siphon. No matter—what I wanted was the engine. When I mounted it on our aluminum rowboat, the craft moved through the water at incredible speed. I could outrace far more expensive, elegant craft with ease.

Living three doors down from us were Gar and Win Wood. Both had been pioneers in building and racing sleek, streamlined-looking mahogany motorboats during the 1940s. Their magnificent speedboats would emerge onto our bay at about dusk, but only when the water's surface was like liquid glass. The deep-throated roar of their Rolls-Royce engines could be heard for miles, it seemed. I often waited for their appearance on those magic evenings. But to me, my metal rowboat, laden with firewood in its front end to help the motor maintain traction in the water, was no less elegant than these regal craft.

We were beginning to play organized team sports. I had become a fairly agile skater, and at five foot seven I would never star at basketball. Sports like swimming and gymnastics were not yet heard of in our school system. I chose ice hockey as my sport and spent countless hours passing and shooting pucks on backyard rinks. Snowdrifts created by our shoveling quickly turned into ice and were our "boards." A neighbor who had played briefly in the National Hockey League became my sometime mentor.

My sports participation was done under a cloud of deceit. One of my childhood operations had been a nephrectomy—a kidney removal. By rights, I had no business playing contact sports. The danger, of course, was possible damage to my remaining kidney. I logically reasoned that I would surely rather die than not participate. So I lied. I lied and hid my scars.

Junior and senior high school brought other opportunities for growth in new extracurricular activities. I sampled all of them. I edited the high school paper for two years, served as president of the thespians, and became a stage actor (skilled in my own mind only). Every fall, several of us gathered to shout Samoan battle cries at football games—we were perhaps the only male high school cheerleaders in the state.

During those halcyon years, success and recognition and their attendant notoriety were simple to achieve. Play by the rules, work harder than anybody else, and success was assured. I proved it to myself beyond a doubt one winter afternoon.

I cut through the gym after hockey practice one evening and fell upon some strangely outfitted folks squaring off against one another with rapiers. They had wire masks on their faces and wore padded white jackets and pants.

"Would you like to join us?"

"What are you doing?"

"It's a fencing tournament. Come on in."

"You bet! How do you *do* this stuff?"

I got a seven-minute crash course in the sport. Then I donned my mask and protective suit. I hacked and thrashed my way through several opponents but was beaten soundly in the end. I learned days later that I had intruded upon the Minnesota State Fencing Championships. I finished the day in third place among the competitors. I never fenced again.

Those most unimpressed were the people I most needed for validation and approval. My father was silent regarding my efforts or my achievements. My mother offered me a "That's nice, dear," then returned to reading her "Minneapolis Star".

But as I think back, Leo was always strangely unwilling to describe *his* experience as a cabin boy in the West Indies or as editor and writer for the literary magazine he and his small band had birthed and nurtured.

As my awareness of Leo's world of words began to expand, I observed a remarkable skill my father possessed, which added to my admiration, envy, and frustration. My homework occasionally required that I seek references for pertinent information. Timidly, I climbed downstairs to learn whether there were any books I could seek information from my father's library. Leo fielded my question, rose from his typewriter, turned, pointed, and walked straight to some volume or other. (He did it in near-darkness, mind you.) He then opened the volume to within pages of the information I sought. While I watched, he pulled another book and another! It often took multiple trips upstairs from the basement to carry all the references he'd provided.

It took decades before I realized my father knew *every* printed word in that vast cave. He was a self-made man of letters. I had missed that talent cleanly in my struggle to get noticed and validated at home.

I had always admired his talent with words and ideas. Leo's advertising creations—with such campaigns as Hamm Brewing Company's forest animals; the electricity industry's Reddi Kilowatt, a helmeted construction belt–clad lightning bolt; and Pillsbury's Doughboy—stood as testimony to his creative mind. He had become a sort of icon in print advertising.

He was also a mentor. On weekends, Leo hosted his "apprentices" to drinks and fishing. When I was in their midst, I could feel the connection and the affection they had for him. I envied them.

Leo was passionate about fishing, and like everything else in his life, it was serious business. He hooked up an ancient freezer in the basement of our house and filled it with critters, fish, and turtles. The porch wall was home to an ever-increasing array of fancy rods and reels, lures, and other toys of the fishing trade.

Leo discovered "fish printing" as a means to preserve his special catches. Imitating an old Japanese art form, he painted a fresh fish with India ink, then covered it carefully with rice paper. When the paper was removed, it boasted a primitive image of his fish. He joked that he could sell prints to proud fishermen who balked at stuffing prized catch and hanging it over the mantelpiece.

The Kennedys' trophy catch was not even a fish. It was a turtle. Leo came across a massive soft-shell turtle as it made its way down the fire lane next to our house. Perhaps it had been on a garbage run or had been egg stealing the night before. Its shell was larger in diameter than a garbage can lid. It had a long, lizard-like neck and an angular, almost prehistoric-looking head. Sporting too-large nostrils at the end of its snout, it was malevolent indeed. It hissed loudly at us and turned slowly to face us. It had no teeth, but its jaws looked razor sharp. A beak-like structure extended from the end of its snout.

And I imagined it said to me, "All the better to hold on to you, dearie, as I tear pieces from your flesh."

Leo shot the creature through the head with a .22-caliber rifle, and we hauled the cadaver to Leo's basement freezer.

But the turtle had its revenge. It survived long enough to bite through an exposed copper pipe, which carried liquid refrigerant. About a week later, a chance entry into the "freezer room" unleashed an effluvia of rotten turtle, fish, game birds, and one or two rounds of Oka cheese (an annual gift to Leo from his father in Montreal). The Oka, crafted by monks somewhere in the Laurentian mountains of Quebec, smelled bad enough when fresh. In the freezer soup from hell, the cheese would have smelled sweet. My father spent a full three days scooping, bailing, and scrubbing. He buried or burned the detritus, every vestige of his collected vittles. It took weeks for the smell to dissipate.

My father loved guns. And like many boys my age, I shared my father's fascination. But we hunted together only once. One autumn morning, we headed for a farmer's woods. We tramped for hours through the brush and mire looking for squirrels. I carried an ancient, single-shot .410-gauge shotgun. Bored and tired, I removed myself from the hunt and took potshots at small birds perched high in nearby trees. The odds that a single pellet would hit one at that distance were small. I was suddenly overwhelmed with shame and remorse when one of my targets actually plummeted to the ground. I rushed to its small carcass, hardly more than a tuft of feathers amid the leaves and twigs on the forest floor. It was a dead starling. I buried it under its tree and put the gun aside. I never fired a rifle again.

My father also introduced me to archery. He had been on outings with his young men several times, but they had bagged no worthy game as yet. Using Leo's bow and equipment, I was quite accurate in my own backyard, but when we hunted, my only "kill" was a tuft of belly hair from a doe. She flipped her white tail at me as she casually disappeared into the woods.

I learned many years later that Leo was not only a lousy shot but was often a danger to his friends. He was prone to gesticulate wildly with his firearm, swinging it recklessly in his comrades' direction, loaded and cocked. It must be said that the group routinely fortified themselves from the cold with generous quantities of bourbon.

My mother's role in my rearing was more complicated. I was a kid growing up in the Midwest. It was commonly assumed that all heaven-bound Minnesotans were either Lutherans or Methodists, else they would fry in hell forever. That fate scared the hell out of me. But I had a hard time resolving the issues of death, spirit, faith, hope, and eternal life as described by my friends. Never having been exposed to such lofty fare at home, I demanded that our family attend a church to get some answers.

In response, my parents agreed to take me to the First Unitarian Church of Minneapolis, where, it has been said, the only time Christ's name was mentioned was when the janitor fell down the stairs. Among my friends, Unitarians certainly did not qualify as heaven-bound Christians. As I grew older and began to prioritize my goals, I gave up their visage of salvation as a lost cause.

It should be clear that I was not raised in a God-fearing house. My Catholic-raised father was, in his words, "A card-carrying atheist."

I knew little or nothing about my Jewish heritage. And I understood even less about Esther's special brand of Judaism. She had been something of a rebel as a young woman. But the family of her childhood was her tribe, her comfort, her solace, and her protected place.

We celebrated Chanukah as our one Jewish holiday. Each year my mother produced two tin menorahs. Each measured three by one and a half inches. We put birthday candles of assorted colors in them and lit one every evening for six days. Each night Deb and I got a nickel. And every year we were told the Jews were God's favorite people because he made the oil last longer than it should have.

Organized religion continued to elude me. The one behavior my parents expected from me was the golden rule. I was told, "Stand in the other guy's shoes for a while, before you make a judgment."

But try as I might, I couldn't understand her life of forced isolation as seen from my mother's shoes. She did not write letters; she rarely phoned her kin. My grandmother flew to Minnetonka every summer at Leo's expense. She stayed with us for three months of each year. Her routine was constant. By day she baked sweets with flaky crusts that were filled with sweet nuts. At night she made it very clear to us kids that she did not like our father much at all. He drank too much. And...I never understood the rest of it, although she repeated it almost nightly. Then she went to bed.

My cousins had all moved to Southern California. It seemed to me the mecca that was Detroit (and all points east) hadn't suited them either. We made several summertime visits by auto when Debbie and I were young. I remember very little of those vacations, except that my mother was giddy with joy at her reunions, and the air in Los Angeles was actually *pink*.

My mother hated to cook. She knew how to create four casseroles. She made massive quantities of each and stored them for eternity in our freezer/porch when the weather was cold. We were treated to roast or steak once or twice a year on random occasions. In late spring and summer, she discovered the first local drive-in restaurant in our area, a drab, brown boxy little building with Snuffy's emblazoned on it in bright yellow, our culinary future was assured! Roasted chicken, picked up from the local grocery chain, was another favorite. The vegetables we ate had invariably been purchased from the grocer's freezer or a can. The only exception was Esther's love of fresh sweet corn. There was plenty of that in Minnesota.

Most important, I did not understand that as the firstborn son of this Jewish mother, I could never receive unqualified approval for any of my efforts or achievements. As a youngster, I longed for a single unsolicited expression of praise: "Good job. I'm proud of you."

I never got it. And it drove me crazy. By the time I understood what had happened and why, my perceived solution was a clean break from the relationships that bound me to my forbears—and a determination not to repeat the errors my folks had made.

Four years my junior, my sister, Debbie, and I had little contact. Our circles never crossed. One day, before I found solace, independence, and power in my rowboat, I was with a friend, and as we were pulling away from our dock. Debbie danced up and down the beach naked, revealing parts of her anatomy that I'd never seen or heard about before! The rationale for that exhibition was both embarrassing and baffling. I never understood it. And I never forgot it..

I *did* know she was as bad in school as I was good. Without exception, after report cards were issued, all hell broke loose in our living room. My grades were never mentioned or discussed. Debbie had flunked everything—again! My father fumed. And bellowed—if he had been carrying the aluminum glass long enough. And the more he raged, the more loudly Esther defended her daughter. It made me crazy! I was jealous of the attention she received. I still remember the vision of Debbie, half hiding behind our mother while she mocked me with weird faces and contortions.

Deb may well have had a learning disorder. Her school nonperformance pattern was repeated over and over. But my perspective was very different. Was Esther using my sister's consistently lousy school performance to goad and punish her husband? She took greater pride in Debbie's failures than my successes; it made no sense.

As I passed from junior to senior high, the diatribes from Esther became alarmingly repetitive, like tape recordings.

At times Deb's grades took second place to money and Leo's extravagant spending on books, guns, and records. After all, report cards were only issued four times a year. These confrontations happened almost nightly!

Over time, Esther's fury devolved from heated anger to an icy, simmering rage. It was hate. And it was constant. She never laughed. Her words were uttered like machine-gun fire. Always attacking; always destructive.

Leo's reactions were rebutted in kind; expressions in fits of explosive rage were followed by his escape to parts unknown. At last, he sought refuge in his basement, where he had gallons of wine, the halo light, Shakespeare or Elizabethan melodies played loud enough to interfere with any other sound in the house, his books, and separation.

And Debbie's crappy grades never improved.

My means of escape became more varied. Sports and extracurricular activities kept me away from home. The more, the better. Keeping ten balls in the air at one time was *fun*. The boat continued to be my salvation until I was fifteen. I was eligible for a driver's permit and then a license. A car brought me more independence, but my patterns of association and escape had been formed long before.

My success bred recognition, only to generate more success, I was a cocky kid and full of myself. When it was time for me to choose a college, I strode into the counselor's office.

"What's the best college?" I demanded.

"Harvard, certainly."

"Where is Harvard, anyway?"

That was good enough for me. I filled out the application and chose the University of Chicago as my backup. The job was done.

When I was accepted, my mother gave me a shrug and a small smile.

"Your cousin Danny received an AP at MIT."

I didn't know what AP meant. Neither did she. My father gave me a one-armed hug and repeated his line about the sixth grade. But *I* was proud of me. I was the first of the Kennedy clan to graduate high school and the first to attend college, let alone Harvard. And I was a hair's breadth away from more freedom than was comfortable.

During the summer after graduation, I hung out with my pals and had my first taste of liquor—peppermint schnapps, and it was awful! I tried to gently disengage myself from the girls I'd chased and won, lost and befriended. I was sent to something called Boys' State in Saint Paul, the state capital. There I was urged to run for (and won) an election for Lieutenant governor—based on what qualities, I never understood. I gave lectures across the state and got to give a penny's worth of teen wisdom to legislative meetings. (I remember little or nothing about those sessions. I am sure my audiences found me just as forgettable.)

Just a week or so before I was to fly to Boston, my half-brother Stephen came to visit. I had spent a week with him two summers before at his home in Montreal: it had been our very first opportunity to spend time together. Fifteen years my senior, he was divorced from his first wife, was dating a woman who looked uncommonly like a bison, and had just recently recovered from fracturing the arches in both feet while practicing ballet barefoot. On this, his first visit to our home that I recall, he demanded to water ski behind my rowboat. I obliged him, but at the expense of my beloved motor, which blew a rod while straining to pull his sorry behind out of the water. At the end of his visit, I confided that I was anxious about attending Harvard College.

His response was, "Yeah. You'll do it Cum Laude."

I never saw or spoke to him again.

Stephen had never attended college. He worked at whatever job suited him until he married. Then he became a laboratory technician at the Royal Victoria Hospital in Montreal. By the time I visited him, he was director of their blood bank. Ultimately, he married again—happily, this time, became very fat, and died instantly from a heart attack at age 60. I learned of his death too late to attend his funeral.

CHAPTER FIVE

The transition from high school hot-shot senior to Harvard freshman was a lot like walking the streets of Cambridge in an autumn rainstorm—the locals called it a nor'easter. The rain blew in sheets, stinging your face and eyes. A wet, icy wind waited for you around corners and then swept out unexpectedly. It could blow you off your feet. Then more rain ripped through your new (and first) fabric raincoat and made a wet rag out of it within minutes. It quickly destroyed the crease in your new gray flannel trousers and drenched your socks. And worst of all, the quaint brick and cobblestone sidewalks of Cambridge, Massachusetts served as tiny reservoirs for rainwater that drenched your feet and quickly rendered your new Weejun loafers beyond repair.

I was reduced to a soggy seventeen-year-old nothing dancing crazily while trying to avoid puddles in America's seat of learning.

My new best friends were now Confused, Bewildered, and Scared to Death. I'd been warned this would happen.

Of course, I was not alone. There were lots like me in every freshman class. I had to quickly define some goals and seek new means of comfort. All freshmen were required to choose or to be assigned to a freshman dormitory within the walls of Harvard Yard. I had requested a public high school student as my roommate. I was interested in American history and in writing. I had been involved in athletics. And I was going to be a physician (although I didn't have the slightest idea why).

My roommate, virtually the first person I met that fall, was Peter, another mid-western kid from my high school athletic conference. His school's hockey team had always pummeled us in the regional tournament.

But this Peter was no jock. Instead, he was a true patrician, the first I'd met, a princely sort who demanded total silence at night—no music or small talk allowed! He slept only in total darkness, with bedspreads under our entrance door and towels over the windows. I stumbled over his books and squash gear to find the bathroom after he retired for the night. He didn't converse—he granted discourse. Our time together, gratefully, lasted only a year. But it was a long one.

We were assigned advisers, generally men who lived in the freshman dorms and knew their charges fairly well. They were generally available to answer questions pertaining to college life. Many interacted with freshmen on a daily basis. Mine was a virtual unknown to me. I met him only once.

"Going into medicine? Go premed. And to boost your chances, take an honors major: American history and literature. You'll get all the stuff you want, like, and need to learn. And wind up with good tickets to boot." I didn't know what he was talking about.

I began attending lectures with over five hundred other students. Some lectures were fascinating and wondrous. I learned about the physiology of vision from the man who "invented" it, Dr. George Wald. He had as much fun talking as I had listening. But there were others—government, calculus, and the like—where I was far more intimidated by the students than by the subject itself.

I sought my comfort zones, stuff I knew about. I played ice hockey and rowed skulls. In the spring, I played on the Harvard golf team and was astounded to note, during our spring trip to sun and grass, that Duke College female undergraduates had shapely ankles, legs, and bosoms. It had been six months since I'd seen those in Cambridge. I considered transferring on the spot.

In truth, I was still scared to death, mostly of those who spoke English, but talked a jargon I could not understand. They colluded with their pals, talking passionately about government, biochemistry, and astrophysics. I escaped to go to hockey practice, or hit golf balls into nets perched a floor above the ice at Watson Rink, or explore the massive expanse of Harvard's graduate schools.

It got easier and easier to skip a meal, and gain an hour of study time. Late at night I rushed to a local fast food place where one could buy an egg, toast, and coffee for thirty cents. When I had cash to burn I bought one of the local legendary roast beef sandwiches.

By early spring, when the mud began to dry, and the grass smelled sweet, my gums began to bleed. The physician at the infirmary told me I had scurvy! Vitamin C deficiency! A disorder, I had long thought, of sailors who had to be at sea for long periods, eating only what they caught in the ocean. And now--me!

Thereafter, I began to care considerably more about what and when I ate.

Toward the end of the school year it was time to join a "House," one of ten or so dorm facilities that offered more room, less austere surroundings, more upscale furnishings, and more freedoms than we'd had as freshmen. My choice was Winthrop House, the jock house, not because I was noteworthy as an athlete, or would ever be, but because I was comfortable with young men who knew and enjoyed the experience and the camaraderie of some sort of team participation and who loved competition. Most of those men became lifetime best friends. I finished the year with B's and a smattering of A's. It was good enough, I guessed, for a kid from the wilds of Minnesota. I finally became convinced I could indeed keep up with these freshman wizards from everywhere—that I might really belong here after all.

I was beginning, just beginning, to have some sense of the need for prioritization in this new world. And then I met Le Marquis de Rothschild.

CHAPTER SIX

I was in a downtown subway station, returning from a date. The underground station was empty. So was my head, I guess, and I was swinging my black needle-nosed umbrella as if it were a golf club. I had just returned from the Harvard golf team's trip to North Carolina, and visions of golf balls soaring into a blue sky occupied my thoughts.

Then from an unknown quarter came the voice of a French male. "Do you have a ball to hit?" Before me was a small, portly man, perhaps five foot two, with coiffed hair, very curled eyelashes, and dark eyes that purely danced. He was dressed in a cashmere blue blazer, the obligatory flannel trousers with a one-inch cuff and creases that could slice bread. His shoes were a golden tan and perfectly polished to a high gloss.

"If this is a pickup, it's a weird one," I thought. He was pleasant and extremely polite, but his interest in me was nonetheless unsettling. It was 1963. I never had considered intimacy with a male, *whatever* his celebrity was. He asked my name. His was Herbert Rothschild.

Medicine Man

Herbert was indeed a member of the Rothschild family. He had come to the United States to make his own way. He ran the romance language program at a private boys' school in Cambridge located near the Charles River as it snaked past the Harvard Undergraduate Houses. He gave me his card. A few days later he called. Would I please join him for dinner?

"What the hell?" I decided. "Unless he packs a razor in those shiny shoes, I can probably deal with anything else he tries to bring to our party."

A week or so later, I was treated to an incredible meal served on sterling silver plates. Just as I was getting wary again, he asked, "I need someone to run my language laboratory at the school. Would you be interested?"

At the time, I had two jobs at Harvard. Both involved running vats of soup, scrambled eggs, or beef stew to the houses' dining rooms from a central kitchen. I rolled my wares on metal carts through an endless maze of underground tunnels to their destination. A language lab sounded like a gift from the gods!

And then, out of nowhere, he added, "I have a dear friend, the Comtesse de D. She has a young son in need of tutoring during the summer. Could you meet with her, as a favor to me?"

Perhaps this was a summer job, too! I met the Comtesse at a coffeehouse the following day. She was a handsome woman of about fifty. And French. (I was beginning to recognize the speech patterns, the liberal use of hands, the voluble indignation hiding just below the surface.) She asked about my interests.. I was open about my rearing, my studies, and my goals.

Then she said, "I have a thirteen-year-old son, not a fine student. He needs work in Latin and mathematics. We will be at Bar Harbor for the summer. We're kind of like a big crowd up there—I have two teenaged daughters who are a handful. My husband occasionally drives up from Boston for the weekend. I love to cook in the French way, so you will eat well. And there are facilities available for sports. My husband has a boat, and he loves to sail about when he's there. Once in a while, I will have a party, and you will meet some interesting people. I'll pay you fifty dollars a week. I'd like you to work with him for two hours a day. It's not much money, but I think you'll enjoy your time there."

Be still, my heart! This was Gatsby revisited on the coast of Maine! I'd barely break even on finances, but the potential for unknown promise was irresistible. So while my classmates worked at construction jobs or sold encyclopedias in poor Boston neighborhoods, I was off to Maine!

During the winter and spring of that year, I took twice-weekly strolls to the Green & Tuppence School for boys. There, I monitored audiotapes and answered the occasional question from the students. Mostly, I studied. It was more gentlemanly than hauling stew through the tunnels that served as the nutritional equivalent of a vascular system for Harvard College.

I returned home in the spring after final exams. Home had changed dramatically in the interval of nine months. It was no longer at Lake Minnetonka. The family had moved back to Homer Street in Norwalk. Leo was sixty-eight years old, and well past the age of obligatory retirement at the ad agency in Minneapolis. Now faced with the financial challenges of a daughter to educate and a wife whose status was still an unknown, he had been advised to leave the home he had rented for the one he owned. For all his married life, Esther had been the money manager. Now, in the face of her obvious inattention to such affairs, and her recent history of offering huge amounts to people she did not know, he had no idea of how to proceed. I wasn't aware of his desperation; I can only guess my father left me out of his crisis, aware somehow that I was surrounded by academic dragons aplenty.

In the spring of 1963, I bought my first car, an aging red Fiat Spyder with a canvas top and thirty-five thousand miles on the odometer. It would be my steed and my talisman as I traveled up the New England coast. I was off to find adventure with golf clubs, a few T-shirts, a change of socks, shaving gear, and my Harvard uniform (blazer, flannels, Weejun loafers—check!). I was off, more than anything else, to escape conflicts at home I did not understand but knew I could not influence.

The trip to the Maine coast was terrific. The weather was cold, and the aura of the place was peaceful. Upon arrival at my employer's home, my first thought was, *"This* is where the rich and famous go in the summer."

I was met by the comtesse. In the hallway, I saw my prospective student race up the front stairs with two young women in angry pursuit. Each outweighed me by about forty pounds, racing and cursing at their brother as they all pounded up the stairs. My fantasies of nubile, adoring teenage daughters vanished in the Maine mist.

"Call me Alicia," said my hostess. "All the other kids do."

After a tour of the house (my bedroom had once been a footman's quarters) Alicia and I sat in the parlor and drank iced tea as we chatted. The home, the grounds, and the Atlantic ocean lapping at the rocks reminded me of Lake Minnetonka gone big time.

My employer's daughters took me on a tour of Southwest Harbor. The "sports" included a short executive golf course and tennis courts, plus a too-cold swimming pool, turned green with algae and inattention. But the "boat" was a forty-odd-foot yacht with its own crew!

When Saturday came, I finally got to meet Alicia's husband. John D. was America born, a bald-headed fellow with an open face and a quiet but hypervigilant manner. He was thick through the chest and abdomen, which had gone to fat. He worked as a stockbroker in Boston, and made the commute to Maine in his Porsche every second or third weekend.

He habit was to drive up the coast Friday night after the stock market closed. The next morning his family, assorted guests, and I sailed the Maine coast, pulled fresh lobsters and clams from fishermen's traps or nets, and ate till forever.

Alicia's parties were grand affairs, with guests literally straight out of *Who's Who in Politics in America*. Averell Harriman, a few Rockefellers, and Dean Acheson were names I recognized. My friend Herbert tripped daintily down the back porch stairs arm in arm with an well-known political satirist of the day. They were clad in matching Speedos.

In contrast, my two hours a day with young Tom were spent in serious study. Whether I did him any good or made his life a little easier, I never knew. If I had spent a fraction more time with him, he may have learned more than declensions and division. I did what I had been hired to do. For the rest, I had my independence—although I loved the occasional spin in my host's Porsche. I was not transformed by rubbing elbows with these hugely rich people. I was a fortunate observer; this was opulence I could absorb only a small swallow at a time. I was too busy trying to identify myself to lust after these folks and their lifestyle.

During my free time, I explored Bar Harbor and the Maine coast, played golf, helped around my hostess' home, ran errands, and prepped pretty assiduously for my tutoring sessions. But overall, it was a summer of extravagance and leisure.

For years, I remarked glibly that during that summer I had access to the mansion, the grounds, the golf course, the car, the yacht, the daughters, and the countess. In retrospect, it was a statement that rolled easily off the tongue. It was improper and disrespectful. But it made a great tale!

Alicia mentioned once or twice in passing that I would be a perfect match for her niece, who lived just outside Paris.

I promptly forgot all about it. I had to prepare for my sophomore year.

Summer was over. It was time to become a grunt, a worker bee. The Fiat found a parking space to hibernate. It had begun to leak oil, but I didn't give it a moment's thought. I moved my belongings into my new digs in Winthrop House.

Academically, I opted to take, in effect, a triple major. History and Literature was an honors major, and selection was limited. The work required was equivalent to completing studies in both fields. Applicants were screened, interviewed, and compared. Many were not accepted. The third, and most frightening area of concentration was premed. It would put me face to face with the death squad of physics, calculus, and organic chemistry—and eyeball to eyeball with a horde of bright, cutthroat men and women whose goal was to knock me on my ass. Hockey, golf, girls, and hanging out with my Winthrop House pals would have to ride in the backseat for a long time.

In late September, I happened upon an invitation to a mixer at Wellesley College, some twenty miles west of Cambridge. Wellesley girls were considered bright and independent but were somehow softer and more approachable than the girls from Radcliffe. It was said they also bathed more often. I'd been to Wellesley a couple of times during my freshman year. My anticipation was to meet a pretty girl I could talk to and snuggle with a bit. That's what I knew experientially.

At the mixer there were hordes of horny young Ivy League men. Some were more awkward in their movements, halting as they approached a girl to talk or dance. Were these the MIT guys, the Tech Tools? Others were far more elegant, sweet smiling, and more clever than I. No matter, I presumed they had hormones too. As at every mixer, the men lined one wall of the large hall, and the Wellesley young women lined the other.

Suddenly, I spotted a small young woman in a Christmas-red dress. Head down, she brushed her hair quickly from her face as she watched her partner's feet, or hers. And then…she glanced up.

And I fell into the greenest eyes I had ever seen.

I asked her to dance. She smiled. Her two front teeth were a tiny bit crooked. Strangely, that added to her beauty. But her smile was brilliant, confident. There was an unsophisticated toughness in her. Her voice was pleasant, soft with a southwestern lilt that could become a real twang on demand. When requested to demonstrate "the cowboy yell," she uttered a soft but enchanting cowgirl "Yee-hah!"

Her name was Anne Davis. She was a sophomore majoring in economics and mathematics. Her home was Carlsbad, New Mexico. She had been a small-town high school graduate like me.

Whatever her studies, her manner was most pleasant. Her voice was calming. She was oh, so pretty. And how I loved those eyes. When she looked at you, they sparkled in an almost phosphorescent way—like looking into deep water. They were inviting in a hugely comfortable but subtly sexual way. I asked her on a date to the next Harvard football game. As we spoke on the phone, I was comfortable in her presence; there was no acting or pretending necessary. Neither of us had anything to prove to the other, except perhaps our mutual attraction.

Three months after I met Anne, I took a fairly savage blow to the head during a hockey scrimmage. Even after a couple of days, I was disoriented to place and direction, and my speech was reduced to a stutter, which lingered for weeks. I went to the Harvard infirmary for help. I was frightened by my injury, maybe for the first time in my life.

\The doctor announced, "You had a concussion! Get over it!"

But he did a physical examination.

"What's that huge scar in your left flank?"

That was the hole left by my absent left kidney. I was caught! The hockey coach sent me a letter suggesting strongly that I should be expelled if I ever set a skate on Watson Rink again.

I felt alone, frightened, and insecure about my health and potential performance for the first time in several years. I wanted comfort and understanding.

My mother had always been incapable of that kind of support. I had never sought comfort from my father.

But Anne was there to offer her company and concern.

It was then that Alicia the comtesse reentered my life. I received a call—she was giving a party at her home, and could I come? I accepted, adding that I wished to bring a friend.

"Of course!"

Within days, I was seated in Alicia D's parlor, Anne at my side, being introduced to the Parisian niece—the one the comtesse had picked for me. The visit itself was pleasant but brief. The atmosphere was frigid and prickly. Alicia called me a week or so later and offered an ultimatum of a prolonged trip to Paris, or my "little Wellesley girlfriend." I answered her on the spot. I never heard from her again.

By the spring of that school year, I raised a ridiculous question. I asked Anne to marry me. She agreed. We would defer marriage until after graduation. Neither of us had planned anything remotely resembling our growing affection. I was in love—forever.

I completed my sophomore year with a decided lack of academic passion. I'd learned it was called "sophomore slump," and I had my share of it, but good. But I'd done fairly well in my premed courses, and…I was in love.

CHAPTER SEVEN

Medical school became a priority as I labored my way through my multiple curricula. I had little time to reflect on my future while spending countless hours poring over Steinbeck, Hemingway, the Puritan Papers, women's suffrage, physics, and organic chemistry. Many evenings, I traveled to Wellesley in borrowed cars, on the MTA, or by hitch hiking if necessary. (The shiny Fiat had given up the ghost.) I became a known quantity at Anne's dormitory. We spent our time in earnest study, but even studying was far more pleasant when I was near her.

Why in hell was I going to be a physician anyway? I honestly had no idea. Years later, a psychiatrist friend suggested the traumas of my first four years forced a kind of "infantile Patty Hearst syndrome" in me. Giants in white masks and gowns kept trying to kill me by cutting me up. It was either "join 'em or die."

The other question was, why fool with a second set of studies that emphasized intensive study of American authors and their place and influence on American culture? That answer was less elusive.

I had learned a little about the craft of writing from my father. In early eighth grade, I got a B- on an English essay. It was my first B—ever! I was incensed! In a rage, I took the paper to my father's inner sanctum. As I carried the paper downstairs, the only light in that massive cave was from the fluorescent circle above his typewriter. Papers were strewn about the floor. The smell of old books, plus the Oka cheese shipped from Canada each Christmas, filled the room. An Elizabethan lute chirped loudly from his phonograph. The room was dark as I descended the stairs. This was Leo's sanctum. We kids didn't go there for fun.

"Dad, I got a B on a composition, and I'd like your help. I think it's okay as it is, but the teacher doesn't like it for some reason. There's a comment there, but it basically says, 'Redo.'"

"Let me look at it." He glanced at the first page, and the second. He drew a diagonal line across each in red pencil.

"Five lines" was all he said about my erudite twenty-five-hundred-word essay! He went back to his work. I was confused at first and defensive as hell. But I was forced to examine the piece critically and examine phrase by phrase what I had written. It stank! The piece was filled with flowery alliterations and metaphors that added nothing to its purpose. It started nowhere and ended nowhere. Grudgingly, I chopped it to pieces and put it back together minus the crap. It was half a page long. Leo took it up, only to mark it to pieces again. In the end, he was almost correct. Seven lines. And only then did he reward me with a smile.

We endured each other thusly for about two years. It didn't matter a hoot that I was Peter Kennedy, son of Leo.

I was a junior-junior apprentice, much inferior in skill and imagination when compared to his doting horde at the ad agency.

I hated that my father—my mentor—was always right about this stuff. I hated that I looked stupid, even dimwitted. I hated the inconsistencies of my thoughts and words. But most of all, I was more *convinced* than ever that I could never have the creative thought, or the facility of subtle expression, or the wealth of words in those thousands and thousands of books that were always *in his head*. I could never wield those tools without a lifetime of experience, imagination, and talent I didn't possess.

But I slogged through my adolescent ego trips and took my medicine. Day after day, week after week. And all the while, I marveled at his precision and economy of word and expression. I carried my father's tutelage to my work in junior high school English. I finished the course with an A. In celebration, Leo invited the teacher to our home for drinks and dinner. He got the poor young man drunk as reward for his efforts in my behalf.

I emerged from that ordeal capable of completing a cogent thought on paper. But unlike my father, I was drawn to American history in contrast to his love for Elizabethan England. America's authors and poets were, for me, a comfortably large sliver of the English literature pie. I was happy, almost confident, in that field. It was to become a comfortable place to hide.

Some years later, I would repeat the same learning process, and the same love-hate relationship, with another mentor as I wrote my first scientific paper of a hundred-odd scientific papers. And it would happen again as I began to explore what was in my own head.

I had assumed my real interest, and whatever "gift" I had, was in the study of American history and American literature. Deep down, I was afraid to fail my expectations of myself. As a consequence, I hid out amid the subjects I knew. I was unsure I had the gumption or the grit I would need to keep up with men and women better prepared and more intelligent than I.

In this mind-set, I was delighted when a universal prerequisite of med school, organic chemistry, was fun! Known as the "premed killer" on campus, it was a huge course filled with physician wannabes like me. However, the subject matter was not about vague abstractions. Chem Twenty, as the course was called, was really about chasing electrons on paper, having a reasonably good memory, and understanding a few basic principles. The concepts themselves were linear and understandable. And I not only understood what was presented, I could sometimes create correct answers by using alternative routes and methods, tricks, or shortcuts my classmates hadn't considered yet!

My hockey and golf careers had been over since Christmas of my sophomore year. I spent my third year at Harvard studying, and wooing Anne.

The following summer, I drove across the country to be with her in Carlsbad, New Mexico during our summer break. I could not be apart from her, or she from me. I spent two months laying corrugated tin roofing (I melted two pairs of tennis shoes) and hauling fire hoses at a public golf course, both in 120-degree heat.

It was also the time for Anne's family to check me over, to assess my assorted character deficiencies. Mrs. Davis generously offered me room and board in the rear of her house. I was scrutinized critically and often. I got to see Anne only when I drove to the Carlsbad Canyon National Park each night at nine to pick her up from work. Her mother flashed the porch light on and off within seconds of our arrival home. My daily routine was to collapse, knowing that death was near, and revive myself to do the same thing again the next day. But over the summer, my tenacity may have proven to Mrs. Davis that I might be worthy of her daughter.

During my senior year, my grades and MCAT (med school preentrance exam) scores were quite good. After working my tail off on my thesis in history and lit, I got two magna readings and a flunk. My typist, Anne Davis, had consistently misspelled Daisy Buchanan's name, which infuriated an emeritus professor assigned to evaluate my thesis, "The Unwritten Short Stories of F. Scott Fitzgerald: Prelude to Gatsby." I graduated from Harvard cum laude as a kid from a town of 1,500 fishermen.

My success at Harvard notwithstanding, I was perpetually uncomfortable in Cambridge. It was the decorum demanded of students that made me so. Approaching a professor required sipping sherry daintily (It tasted like Karo syrup!), offering abstruse objections to inane, arse-kissing comments by one's colleagues, and the like. The key to success was to get *noticed*, and I was not good at it. I needed to get *out* of the Ivy League for a while. I had no problem interacting with my *really* bright classmates, who were enraptured amid a universe of astrophysics and string theory, concepts I'd neither hoped nor wished to understand. My insecurities stemmed, not from lack of intellect or achievement, but from *feelings*.

I applied to a handful of medical schools. I was waitlisted, and later accepted, at Harvard, but I wanted to be as far as I could from those Harvard premed harpies. New York University appeared almost magically on my list of applications. Harvard College had chosen NYU for me. It was the program my premed advisory committee had recommended for me. But I hadn't seen a premed representative since November of my freshman year. In truth, I had forgotten he existed. If he hadn't picked New York and NYU, who had? And why?

There was only one way to know for sure. I scheduled an interview. Upon my arrival, New York City appeared scarier than Boston, primarily because it was filled with New Yorkers—*loads* of them The dean of admissions at New York University College of Medicine showed me around. He casually mentioned that I'd be paid $14,000 a year for going to school. I was, of course, planning to enter the combined degree program at NYU, was I not?

That was crazy! A combined degree? I didn't know such a thing existed, or why I should want it. I was likely going to squeak through basic science portion of any medical school curriculum, I didn't know the slightest thing about research, and all I wanted was to fix broken bones!

My hosts were crestfallen. Apparently, NYU's professorial program was the path I had been primed for by some unknowable, hidden force at Harvard.

It'd have been really cool if someone had let me know about it. I was furious on the trip home.

"Somebody's going to *pay* me to go to med school? *Impossible!* And why sneak it up behind me like this?" My distrust of the Ivy League went up another three notches.

Ironically, my path in medicine was for many years a perfect parallel of somebody's vision.

I visited Baylor College of Medicine in Houston, Texas. That was as far west as I dared to go! Everybody knew that Californians smoked pot and had wife-swapping orgies. Anne and I feared for our children, not yet more than a gleam in our eyes. They would fall prey to a cult or to the drug culture!

The dean received me warmly. He dismissed my non-science background with a wave of his hand. He had high hopes for his next entering class. (In fact, the class of 1970 had the third-highest MCAT scores in the nation, behind Johns Hopkins and Yale.) The Texas Medical Center itself was a big, sprawling complex. The weather was warm. I was greeted with "Howdy" and "Hi, ya'll" and "Come back and see us real soon." I felt briefly exhilarated. I could be comfortable here!

Anne calmed me when I flipped out periodically over the prospect of medical school. But we'd discussed all this. It was somehow easier to "just do it" when she was around.

I prepared for my graduation, as Anne did for hers. Then we separated for a time while she readied for the wedding in New Mexico and our trip to Baylor in Houston. It was the home of Michael DeBakey, one of the few names in medicine I knew about.

I had *absolutely* no idea of what I was getting myself and my bride into.

We were married in Carlsbad. Several of my pals from college joined me there. Many had become close friends with Anne over our three years as virtually constant companions.

We honeymooned at the Wagon Wheel Inn, outside Carlsbad. My Fiat had morphed into a Corvair Monza convertible—without air conditioning (an unwise decision for Houston and New Mexico, but a pretty typical one for me).

From Carlsbad, we drove south and east toward Houston, through the biggest sky I had ever seen. Ever protective of the people and toys I held dear, I was afraid to drive up to Pike's Peak, because the altitude might damage my air-cooled engine.

We stayed in motel cabins that provided stocked ponds where we could catch trout for our dinner. The saving in dollars was worth the extra effort.

At night, we reveled in our love, our freedom, and our paired destiny—that is, before the temperature dropped to thirty-five degrees.

We were off to a race with multiple unknown, invisible finish lines!

When medical school and the demands of starting an independent life began, I had little contact with my folks for over five years. Leo was sixty-eight, well beyond the obligatory retirement age at his ad agency, and they put him out to pasture. My father sent word to his tutees and learned about a position at *The Reader's Digest* in Pleasantville, New York. The new work site was auspicious. It was reasonably close to Norwalk and the old Homer Street homestead. I was astounded to learn that Leo and Esther were returning to the house they *owned* and were leaving the home they had rented for a decade.

The *Digest* was not concerned about his age as long as he could be productive. And he was productive. He convinced *Reader's Digest* enthusiasts that they needed the best waltz music in the world, the greatest concertos, the greatest symphonies, etc. The company made money hand over fist.

Apart from occasionally fishing in Long Island Sound, Leo's pattern at home was unchanged. He returned from work, prepared his evening meal, retired to his study, drank cheap wine by the gallon, and typed wondrous prose with those same two fingers. And the rafters shook with sounds of Shakespeare at max volume.

Deb was in high school and should have been preparing for college as I graduated from Harvard. She was anything but prepared. Her grades still scraped along at rock bottom. Yet she was blissfully unconcerned about her performance or her future. Tragically, her mother was equally unworried. At the advice of his colleagues, Leo enrolled Deb into a private girls' high school in Darien. The Cherry Lawn School would prepare her for junior college, where she could find focus and then undertake her university training.

It never happened. Deb did attend the Cherry Pit, as Leo called it. And graduated. And then she was enrolled in not one but seven junior colleges in the area. Each institution, in turn, was happy to receive her as long as she was accompanied by her first year's tuition and board.

Her pattern was consistent, to our father's dismay. Debbie called her mother about two weeks after her arrival at each school. (I have a recollection that she was relatively happy at one of them for six weeks. Leo desperately hoped that this was going to be "it"!) She complained bitterly that her classmates didn't like her, or the teachers were cruel, or her room was too hot. On two occasions, she simply left the place, came home, and refused to return.

Leo had done all he knew to do. His children must have the opportunities he never had. And yet he couldn't get it done. For her part, Esther was sure that something would fall into place soon. Her daughter was just a "late bloomer." The pressures of age, time, and money were irrelevant to the woman who had once managed the family's books like Bartleby.

Debbie lived at home for five years. Likely, she was Esther's near-constant companion. In 1970, she married an ex-marine corporal. Jack Rawling, following his separation from the Corps, had begun a career as an airline ticket host. At their wedding, my older daughter Martha placed single flower petals with precision as she preceded Debbie and Jack down the aisle.

Esther continued her slow slide into her special kind of madness. I had seen her at my college graduation. The poor woman had no idea where she was or why she was there. My father was uncommonly patient with her and seemed not to notice her memory or behavioral lapses. When Anne and I joined my parents for a celebratory dinner, Esther launched into an attack upon her husband… again. She had been kidnapped to the Midwest, away from the *real* cultural center and her family (who had all moved to Southern California).

My mother could still be cordial and engaging at times. She was eager to enter political discussions. She defended her positions well, and there were often factual data behind them. But one had to have heard those arguments before to recognize the information was always the same.

CHAPTER EIGHT

The honeymoon had been brief. We both had giants to slay. I was to begin a career with an absolutely unknown end point. Anne, ever practical and organized, was to interview for a job as a programmer. With our few possessions in tow, we arrived in what was then southwest Houston, home of the Texas Medical Center. We looked forward to a future filled with love, performance, and excellence...and we had not a pot to piss in.

And then one of the most important events of my life hit me like a tidal wave.

We had jut moved into our second-floor apartment of the McGregor Arms, a complex about a mile from the Texas Medical Center. Anne was job hunting—her math skills quickly led to her becoming a pioneer in computer language and its application. I hopped into my snappy car and drove to the med school. I bounded up the stairs and was met by a smiling fellow with a big space between his front teeth. (He would later be recognizable as the bureau chief of the local FBI.) Behind him stood a man with thinning, slicked-back hair in a knee-length laboratory coat that said Dean...something on it. He had pursed lips, out-of-fashion eyeglasses, and no suntan. I did not see him smile that day. In fact, I would *never* see him smile during my first five years at Baylor.

But all that escaped me on this day. I raced up the steps, pulled open the heavy glass doors, and was met by a blast of frosted air. I was oblivious to the fact that it was ninety degrees outside with 90 percent humidity at 8:30 a.m. I announced, "I'm Kennedy. I'm here to sign in, or whatever."

"We're so glad," said the gap-toothed guy. "Sign here, and we'll get you a mailbox."

On the way out, I spied my mailbox. There was a copy of a recent *JAMA*—a popular medical journal usually sent free to all med students in the United States. The guy who had just graduated had left it behind.

I stole it. Drove home. Ceremoniously opened to the first page...and could not understand the first word of the advertisement on the inside cover.

My blood ran cold. I was pallid and sweating. I felt faint. I was totally unprepared for a future I had already cast in stone!

Then I had an idea.

Salvation may be at hand!

I drove back to Baylor and bought the thickest medical dictionary on the bookstore shelves.

I raced back to the ceremonial execution desk. Opened the book. And I could not understand the first word of the *definition* of the word I didn't know.

Now I was in full panic mode! No one could ever know how little I knew! Not my wife. Certainly not parents, in-laws, or friends. I couldn't see the dean. He was the guy who couldn't smile!

My life passed before my eyes. I panicked. Then I had what may have been my first and only moment of clarity in my nearly twenty-one years. At Harvard, I had taken a class on intensive reading—not just reading, but *really* reading. Digging to find hidden meaning, or intent, or submerged themes. The objects of the study included Shakespeare, Steinbeck, Fitzgerald, Faulkner, and others. We often spent a week dissecting a single page.

Why could I not, then, memorize, internalize, understand, and explain cogently every word that was relevant to the material I had to learn. I would make each fact or experimental observation part of the fiber of my life.

Lucky for me, I had no idea how long the list of topics was. But it didn't matter. If I worked hard enough and long enough, if I concentrated on one subject to the point of completely understanding it, I had only to go on to the next unknown, because they were *all* unknowns. If I proceeded to the next and the next…I would ultimately come back to the beginning! And presumably learn the totality of medicine.

The only thing it demanded was effort.

So my path was set. The way was clear. All I had to do was start with nothing, learn everything, never forget it, and come back to the beginning.

There were a few bumps early on. The unsmiling dean—none other than Dr. Michael DeBakey himself—told me in no uncertain terms that married students never did well. The demands of their married lives were simply too distracting. This was a time for dedication to one thing! Study! Add children, and nobody completed the race. (I didn't mention this prediction to Anne till years later.)

Measuring our performance as students was a mystery in itself. Class rank was supposed to be hidden from us forever. We were only to focus on our objective: how to become physicians. We later learned that our rank could be somehow "leaked" to us if we were persistent at seeking it.

My objective was a little different. My ranking meant nothing. I simply *had* to learn *everything*. While my classmates studied lecture notes on the brachial plexus (the nerves and vessels in the arm pit), I was trying to understand why the kidneys worked, or the fine anatomy of the hand. I had arrived at each of these incredible adventures by chasing definitions of single words. And through it all, something worked. I fairly loved it—every word, every concept. With agonizing slowness at first, each tiny puzzle piece of knowledge had its own precise place. Words became tissues, organs, concepts, and molecules. There was no end to it. But it didn't matter. I expected none. Over time, questions from my classmates that I didn't understand became recognizable and then *explainable*. And I was often doing the explaining.

There was a bonus: at the end of my freshman year, I was ranked tenth in a class of eighty-four, which itself had ranked third in the nation in entrance examination (SAT) scores. (From then on, I ranked first among my classmates for four consecutive years.)

This process of learning and understanding was like a first kiss and a first roller-coaster ride all blended together.

It was *all* fun. I felt an incredible exhilaration that went on and on!

I bought book after book with money I didn't have. When I found a word I didn't understand, I pursued it till I did. When I slept, I dreamed about molecular and anatomic three-dimensional relationships. I often "sat" on a theoretical organ deep within the body, and I could visualize the organs around it.

I placed myself on top of the duodenum (the small intestine as it leaves the stomach). The liver was up and to the right. The biliary tract trailed downward behind me and entered the duodenum just at my feet. I applied the same visionary principle to molecules of glucose, enzymes, or strands of DNA.

When I prepared for each examination, I considered myself ready if all I did not know could be reduced to one side of a three-by-five-inch card. If I didn't know something, I started over again. During my nightly study jags, I lost all sense of time. There was only information. And amazingly, most all that information has stayed somewhere in my head despite passage of five decades and near-fatal brain trauma.

I used that same information daily to talk to patients, families, and physicians. But at the time, I was confident in what I carried inside my brain and was eager to put it to practical use as a physician.

My first day's terror kept me humble and grateful. I had been so close to total failure. But my learning technique served me well. I understood everything being taught in class, but I was many times out of sync with the professors.

I was engrossed in neurochemistry while the professors lectured on the gross anatomy of the foot.

Students interviewed and examined living, breathing patients during our second year at Baylor. I was supremely rewarded that what I'd learned was relevant to patients on a daily basis. I was in seventh heaven!

In the 1960s the medical school curriculum was standard across the United States. Two years of preclinical study was followed by two years that involved direct patient care. Baylor was fairly unique in that students were encouraged to be involved with patients and their care as early as possible.

Several of us spent time hanging around the ward or in the ER at the Ben Taub General Hospital. On one occasion, the medical chief resident regarded my frequent presence with some interest. (I had no idea what a chief resident was or what he did.) He called me to him and handed me a three-inch needle in a green plastic tube. Then he pulled the curtains around a gunshot-wound victim who had just died.

"This is a spinal needle. You get one stick and fifteen seconds to find the subclavian vein. If your first try misses, you're done. I can't explain to an upset family why there are a bunch of tiny holes under some poor dead guy's collarbone."

I was shown the technique on the recently deceased.

"See? Find the anatomic landmarks, estimate the depth of the vein as it runs under the collarbone, and do it! Remember. Fifteen seconds. Or you're toast."

I knew precisely what nerves and vessels crossed above the first rib and under the clavicle and what their relationships to each other were—I had visualized myself standing there! Pushing the needle ever so slowly, I felt a pop and saw blood flowing from the end of the needle. I quickly removed the needle and applied pressure over the tiny hole. There was no leakage. The man's heart was stopped, of course. *My heart raced, however. This had been more exciting than a hole in one!*

I figured out that when prowling the emergency room, a show of interest, if pursued long enough, could result in learning to start an IV and, if the place was busy enough, in stitching together a superficial laceration.

At the Ben Taub Hospital, every week was a banner week for trauma of every sort. Vehicle accidents, fights with assorted weapons, crashed motorcycles, murder and mayhem among the city's gangs—the Taub was ready for them all. Most ER patients received emergency treatment and were wheeled off to the ICU or to the ward. But a few did not survive or had arrived in the ER as a DOA. I quickly gained confidence and competence with the subclavian stick, a procedure I would use for decades.

The senior resident presided over as many as thirty major trauma cases in a twenty-four-hour stretch. Generally, they were clustered between 8:00 p.m. and 3:00 a.m. Those were the hours of the gunfighters. Young men, usually African American or Hispanic, were brought in by ambulance or car following shootouts in the Fifth Ward, a poverty-marred, gang-infested ghetto not far north of the medical center and the general hospital. There were shootings over turf, women, drugs, or sometimes nothing at all, it seemed.

Communication was pretty terse in the shock rooms— operating suites outfitted to receive major trauma cases.

Everyone's tasks were clear. The initial evaluation was constant, quick, efficient. If a patient was breathing normally, the nursing staff quickly cut off all clothes and surveyed chest, back, neck, head and extremities for signs of trauma or bleeding.

A penetrating wound to the abdominal cavity by a knife or a bullet meant the patient was immediately OR bound to look for damage or perforation of the intestine, and spillage of bacteria-laden intestinal contents into the abdominal or pelvic cavity. A wound in the chest meant possible lung collapse or uncontrolled hemorrhage. Such a patient required immediate evaluation, including a search for signs of other injury, and placement of an IV for medicine delivery or increasing intravascular (within blood vessels) volume.

Placing a chest tube was paramount if the patient was short of breath following a chest wound. Surgical residents, if they weren't busy in the operating room, pushed a sharpened sterile tube into the space between the lung and chest wall. The tube's free end was connected to a source of continuous suction. Air, blood, pus, or serous (yellow) fluid each had a different significance. The information retrieved from analysis of the fluid helped define the cause of the abnormal collection.

I recorded other things in my mind. A man was brought to the ER following massive trauma to his brain. He was dying before our eyes. Nothing could be done. The visage of the resident's face remained with me. He was a tall, scruffy-looking, sleep-deprived fellow. And he had a haunted look in his eyes. It was his eyes I remembered. It had been his job to quickly decide whether to attempt hugely heroic treatment to save, or to extend, the man's life, or to let him die.

Although I had no inkling of it then, I would feel the pain in that resident's eyes a thousand times.

I was enraptured by the wonder and the drama of clinical medicine off and on the wards. I wanted to do forever whatever I was assigned to do that day. I studied day and night.

How did my family tolerate my extramarital love affair with my studies of medicine? I am sure that, even at my best, I wasn't easy to live with. I was cranky, tired, surly, and preoccupied. We had no extra money for gifts or goodies, as we were paying tuition, books, rent, and food on Anne's salary as a programmer doing statistical analysis of cancer clinical trials, plus whatever I could make on the side.

Our first, and perhaps the only knock-down, drag-out fight of our marriage (which is now approaching fifty years) was over the cost of a jar of mayonnaise Anne had brought home from the store.

"It's not in the budget!" I screamed.

Anne wept.

"It was a present for you."

We kept the mayonnaise.

Our first daughter, Martha, was born in the spring of my freshman year. Anne had two maternity dresses that she had crafted herself. I marveled at her ability to pursue her career and run our household while looking as big as a house. Martha's birth was uncomplicated, but molding of her skull while in her mother's pelvis made her head look frighteningly misshaped. Nonetheless, she was a lovely, flaxen-haired baby with all her fingers and toes who cried all night, every night, for ninety-one days. I endlessly walked her at night, cooing and reciting anatomic relationships or biochemical formulae. On the ninety-second day, Anne's mother visited. She cradled her new grandchild for a moment. The crying stopped, and Martha became a normal baby. Anne had returned to work. Almost magically, she somehow found a giant of a woman named Odessa who had a loving touch and the patience of Job to care for our firstborn.

As Martha grew, I spent every possible minute marveling at her and her mother. On one occasion when she was about six months old, Martha suddenly came up onto her knees and her outstretched arms, and crawled a distance of several feet. We were astonished at her precocity! Then she slowly sank to the floor and didn't move another inch for three months.

I worked two to four twelve-hour shifts on a weekly basis, from 6p.m. till morning, at the MD Anderson Hospital Tumor Institute, which was, at that time, a single hospital across the street from Baylor. I ran the clinical laboratory. I did blood counts and serum electrolyte levels. I crossmatched blood and platelets and drew ten thousand blood cultures from cancer-ravaged patients. It was an incredible learning adventure. And it helped feed the family. During residency and fellowship, I frequently moonlighted at neighboring community hospitals.

Baylor offered a teaching program for a small handful of second-year med students. They taught gross anatomy, neuroanatomy, pathology, and histology to the freshmen while doing original research, in addition to carrying a portion of the normal second-year schedule. In return, they received a modest stipend. I leaped at the chance. I could learn, teach, and help provide for my family! Equally important, I was already in love with basic research. By the end of my second year, I had completed a Master's thesis on intracellular organelle study in mouse liver tumors and presented a paper on the previously unrecognized mechanism of action of the enzyme fumarate hydratase. I assisted the man who was among the first to assay for unmetabolized fatty acids in the aortas of patients with atherosclerosis, coronary disease, and aneurisms. Were these substances contributing to plaque formation? We tried to find the answer. Whether I was included in a publication was unimportant. I just loved doing the stuff! All of it! Any of it!

And my family? Anne knew when I was with Martha, and later Sara, I was totally immersed in their excitement, growth, disappointments, and even their fits of protest or anger.

A few years later, as a first-year resident at Yale, I taught Martha to ride her bicycle. White gold hair streaming behind her, head over the handlebars, jaw set, she wore first an expression of uncertainty, then fear, then determination, and at last joyous victory—all in the space of minutes. For my part, I tried hard to make what little free time I had with the girls of the highest quality. At other times, I fell asleep with my face in the stew.

The real backbone for organizing and running the household, arranging for baby care while we worked, grocery shopping, bill paying, and all the rest went to my wife. And somehow, through it all, she loved me.

My first clinical rotation was with a professor in medicine and pharmacology who was renowned for eating med students for breakfast. It usually took about five minutes to devour someone's knowledge base, and seconds more to reduce one's ego to a smudge. Students were to present each case we were following with the resident staff and then answer questions about our basic fund of knowledge and its clinical relevance in the presence of our professor. We assembled in a small conference room, notes in hand. The first student went belly up in about three minutes. The second, a female Texas native, was tremulous and frightened. She went down in two. I was third in line.

For whatever reason, our exchange lasted for over two hours and was finished when Dr. Lang announced that he had a lunch date and was late. I later learned that this man, a zoot-suited slender man of about forty-five, had been a kind of boy wonder during the early days of the National Institutes of Health (NIH). He was often pedantic, off putting, and foul mouthed. But his brilliance was unmistakable. At the end of our four-week rotation, he announced that I must work for him as a fellow. I was too honored, embarrassed, and humbled to say no. And so I gave my word.

But on a day-to-day basis, I loved everything I did or read about. I longed to become whatever topic I studied: cardiac surgeon, nephrologist, pulmonologist, intensive care specialist, oncologist. I moved through my clinical rotations, examining and helping care for an incredible variety of patients.

But none taught me more than a chicken plucker named Fae Longo.

CHAPTER NINE

My first surgery rotation sent me to the Ben Taub Hospital again. Some members of the teaching staff had heard about me, a bright, brash kid who wanted to have his hands in everything. Their instructions to their chief residents were to keep me out of the operating room because I likely would not become a surgeon as a career choice. I was given a project that kept me out of the OR and probably out of their collective hair.

I was assigned to care for Fae Longo. Ms. Longo was a five-foot, 350-pound chicken plucker who had collapsed in her henhouse on the outskirts of Houston. She had reportedly lain with the chickens for three days before somebody found her and had her transported—windows open—to the hospital. On admission, she had evidence of a recent heart attack with attendant heart failure, plus some sort of acute surgical abdomen. Her blood work showed that she was in kidney failure, and her blood sugar was sky high, a consequence of her untreated diabetes. Her lungs were stiff with water, and she had fluid collections in both chest cavities. She was, of course, covered from crown to toe with chicken excrement and feathers. Who was on first or second base was irrelevant. All her crises had to be addressed at once.

Hello, Fae Longo.

The surgical resident approached me in ICU, chuckled, and said, "Good job, Doctor! Doctor Kennedy, is it? May I call you Peter? I'm Bud Grolinger. We've heard a little about you!" He cocked his head and offered me the first hint of a smile I'd seen from him all night. Then he slapped the operative note form, anesthesia records, and emergency room physician's hen-scratched, bloodied admission note into my palm. It said exactly what I reported above. No more. No less.

"She's all yours, Doctor Kennedy!" He turned on his heel and strode off to make rounds, or sleep, or drink a sip of coffee before taking on the next catastrophe. He stopped and cocked his head again. I noted fleetingly that he had a long, lonely forelock of sandy hair that hung nearly to his eye.

"Fix her!" He spun again and strode off.

My first thought was "*Both* of us are as good as dead!"

She required immediate intubation, cardiac shocks to restart her heart, placement of a catheter to drain her urine (there was none), and insertion of large-bore IV needles to pour fluids into her. I watched this intently, wondering where I could begin and what I could do to help save Fae's life. My head seemed suddenly stuffed with useless information about the body. I'd never even started an IV.

As it turned out, I got a brief reprieve. To our collective amazement, Fae's condition stabilized while I was busy measuring her IV fluid replacement rate and her urine flow (still zero) every ten minutes. I didn't know what else I could contribute. By the wee hours of the next day, on IVs, blood products, wide-spectrum antibiotics—and in kidney, lung, and heart failure—she was taken to surgery to explore her abdomen.

I put on my green pajamas, mask, hat, and booties and followed her gurney into the OR. I'd been standing at Fae's bed for eight hours. I called my wife of a year and told her excitedly I was involved in something "really big." I'd be home as soon as I could.

Fae Longo in the operating room was an unforgettable experience. She smelled badly enough after three days with her chickens, but I was unprepared for the smell of dead bowel, feces, and pus floating like soup, lapping against the inside of her belly wall. I was astonished at the skill of the surgical resident, who was able to identify healthy and dead bowel. He showed me that her pancreas had partly digested itself. He then washed the abdomen with endless amounts of sterile water and reconnected the apparently healthy ends of intestine. (The small bowel was shortened to half its length. The colon was brought through the abdomen as a colostomy.) I watched it in absolute awe.

This gruesome scene formed the nexus of my care for Fae Longo. Postoperatively, she remained unresponsive, on a respirator, and with tubes exiting or entering her from every direction. It still all looked Greek to me.

But Fae Longo did not die. She had been placed under my care. I bloody well owed it to her and to me to do my best. After 6:00 a.m. morning rounds, I retired to her bedside and spent most of every day and night redressing her abdominal wound, which had dehisced (come apart) because of infection in the soft tissues. The dehiscence was facilitated by her enormous girth and the great pressures required to inflate her lungs twelve to twenty-four times a minute. I spent entire days, nights, and weekends tending to her infections, lung and kidney failure, renal dialysis, and her failing heart. I kept meticulous records of blood test results, respirator settings, dialysate fluid, and mineral concentrations. I administered fluid and monitored antibiotic choices and fluid volumes both into her and out of her. When I was over my head or confused or felt stupid (I was frequently all three), I could usually find Grolinger. He often gave brief or cryptic answers to my questions.

"Should I try to get rid of some of her lung water, and her effusions, to make the respirator-driving pressures lower?"

He gently and patiently responded, "Yes-s-s." Then it was up to me to figure out how to do it, and at what risk. Should I remove fluid from her pleural cavity, or alter the sodium and bicarbonate concentrations in her dialysis fluid? Should I administer a massive dose of a powerful diuretic? I considered these options and tried to predict their consequences. On this occasion, I removed fluid from her chest cavity with a needle. She improved, but the fluid promptly returned. So I placed my first chest tube, a half-inch plastic tube inserted between the ribs and into the space between the lung and chest wall. I was fearful about lacerating the lung, or the potential for infection. But Fae had shown me it needed to be done. The fluid reservoir indicated that there was two and one half liters of fluid in the chest cavity. But her blood pressure dropped. I then increased our delivery of I.V. fluids and albumin, a plasma-expanding protein, and the pressure rose again. Thus the process continued. I strove to find a balance among the myriad of contributors that would give Fae a chance for recovery.

The ICU nursing staff was patient and even personable with me at first. Somehow the nurses knew that whatever I did correctly, they wouldn't have to repeat later. Besides, they'd seen it all a hundred times and had handheld thirty of me through the procedure in the past.

As I faced the fears of what I didn't know, made decisions, and either lived with my mistakes or tried to repair them, the crucible that was Fae Longo got easier to hold close to my heart. This was not rocket science! There were few true mysteries. I learned that there were two kinds of medical emergencies: the one that had already happened and could likely not be undone, and all the rest. And they could virtually all be approached in the same way. Collect what information you can as quickly as you can and as aggressively as you must. Then determine your options based on the data. And *act*.

As time passed, Fae became my laboratory and my battlefield, where I learned strategic calculation, anticipation and prediction of each crisis, and what I could actually control in my single patient. I learned enormous amounts about acute trauma and about multiple-organ and system failure, skin care, intravenous nutrition, and systemic infection treatment. From my naïve, limited perspective, I was sure that if I could get her lungs, kidneys, heart, and gastrointestinal tract to work again, and if I could get her anterior belly wall to scar in enough to hold her together when she sat or stood, she would have a chance to survive. We'd be in Fat City!

And about three and a half months later, Fae Longo left the hospital. She was still wrapped in a linen bandage, which helped hold her belly together. But the belly wall had essentially regrown upward from the base of her wounds, forming a scar that bound her abdominal wall together (a healing process called secondary intent).

She later underwent skin grafting to cover the area. And I had nursed every damned cell in her belly, gut, kidneys, and lungs back to health. And a couple of bed sores too! I was on cloud nine, full of myself for my efforts but hugely grateful for what I had learned and for the labors I had performed in her behalf.

She returned to the hospital within weeks, however.

Her tracheostomy tube, and in particular the balloon used to prevent air from escaping around it, was essential to expanding her lungs and getting adequate oxygen to her tissues. Her great weight, and the binder that held her belly together, were forces that resisted that expansion. The balloon caused inflammation and subsequent scarring and narrowing of the trachea itself. Sadly, this had occurred at the level of her larynx, which we had predicted, and lower down her trachea, where the air tubes to each lung bifurcate (divide). She died of respiratory failure—asphyxiation, really. I had left the rotation, but her doctors were unable to open the narrowed trachea or to make a new opening lower in the trachea (where it passed beneath the breastbone) to allow her to breathe.

The lessons I learned from Fae Longo reached far beyond my fears, insecurities, and expectations. I had faced extraordinary medical and surgical crises occurring together, then separately, and then together again, or in some new combination. And my patient and I had survived. The approach to every emergency was logical and reflexive. Quickly collect whatever data may be available. Consider risks and benefits. Then act as best you know how. Sitting on one's thumb could be not only painful but dangerous.

Dr. Grolinger never said anything, in the manner of Baylor professorial surgeons. He made not a sound as Fae walked to the van that would move her to a nursing facility. But he was there.

While I labored over Fae, I had my spies as well. Once or twice a day, he'd check with the charge nurse in the ICU. He was usually smiling when he cocked his head and spun on his heel, in his way.

I had never considered it at the time, but the financial cost of her care had been extraordinary. I had attended her from four to thirty-six hours at a time at no charge because I was a medical student. I owed *her* for my experience— more than I could pay. But what about when my care of her had required the presence of an ICU nurse or a physician? She was operated on multiple times. Her dead bowel required at least two trips to the OR. She needed placement of shunts for dialysis, plus frequent replacement of endless tubes and catheters. She was continuously on a respirator support for two months. I later learned the costs in personnel and apparatus, hugely expensive medicines, X-rays, dressings, anesthesia, etc., that went into each procedure. Then after all we had offered her to extend her life, we managed only to cause her death as an untreatable complication of her original illness.

Nonetheless, I received an incredible gift from Dr. Grolinger *and* from Fae Longo. That experience, more than any other medical training, helped cast me into what made me go, and what made me stop, and what made me continue to care for the desperately sick. And what made me write about it today.

CHAPTER TEN

Not every experience during my years of training dripped with gore or immediate drama. Late one night, I was called to see a young woman with an obvious bacterial pneumonia. She was too sick to send home, so I admitted her to the inpatient service and went through the usual drill of culturing her blood and sputum, treating her infection, giving her supplemental oxygen, allaying her anxieties, and allowing her to rest and recover. As was my custom, I visited her bedside at least twice a day to monitor her recovery. It was purely routine. I saw twenty of her a month.

What I had not counted on was her fear. She was a previously healthy young woman who was absolutely certain she would die from her illness.

She recovered, pretty much on schedule and pretty much as one would predict.

But when I prepared to send her home, she proposed a debt of gratitude I had never received before, or since.

"I can't thank you enough for what you did for me," she gushed.

"It was pretty routine, but I'm grateful for you're being grateful. It means a lot. Sometimes we get so wrapped up in our routines that we forget there's a patient on the other side of the bed."

"No! I'm serious. If there's anything that I or my family can do for you, you just have to let me know."

I gently pushed my point. "If you feel worse, or you have more cough or trouble breathing, just call me." I gave her my home phone number, as I would do thousands of times.

"No! No! You don't understand. If you need something taken care of, I can help," she insisted.

"My life is pretty tame," I coaxed. "You just keep getting better. You'll be fine."

"You don't understand! My brother's in the *business*!" She was insistent. "If you need anything—if you need anyone taken care of—I can make a call, and it's done!"

There it was. I would care for thousands of different folks, each with their own story, history, and frame of reference. It was a lesson I never forgot.

I put her chart away and signed the discharge order.

There were other bizarre stories of Texas-style justice. During my first day in histology class, I learned that the classmates to my right and to my left carried pistols in their cars—duly licensed, of course.

While on ER duty as a med student, I cared for an old woman who had been beaten and robbed by an intruder who entered her home through a second-story window. Because she lived in the outskirts of the city, the police could not assure her of a rapid response time. So they gave her a .410 shotgun and a single cartridge to use if she was attacked again. Sure enough, the burglar made a second attempt at entering the same window. The old woman fired her single round at what she could see—the man's head and neck. The birdshot in her weapon didn't kill the man, but it left him blind and severely scarred for life.

    Apart from my abhorrence of my pistol-packing classmates, I came to love the immediacy and inherent risks of treating major trauma cases. That was due, in part, to the immediacy of necessary medical treatment and the courage to make decisions quickly, and then act on them. I was becoming an internist who thought like a surgeon.

CHAPTER ELEVEN

As I have said, during my rotations through nephrology (kidney disease), cardiology, and other medical subspecialties, I was totally captivated by facing clinical situations that demanded rapid collection of a database of information followed by assertive, sometimes aggressive action. CAT scans were certainly available, but I often got answers from patients simply by listening to their story and examining them carefully. Often, X-rays, lab studies, and scans only confirmed what the patient had told me already.

My favorite time in the hospital was between 8:00 p.m. and midnight. There were no staff and administrative types to bar my way, and I could search the hospital for information I needed. There was no waiting, no hedging, no fussing. Data was retrievable, or it wasn't. A throat swab and examination of the predominant bacteria was a two-minute process. An X-ray or scan could be cajoled out of the technician and reviewed within a few minutes. *And* I could examine the data and draw conclusions myself. I was in my element. And time was nonexistent. I was through with a job only when it had been completed to my satisfaction and to the patient's benefit.

During my rotation through pediatrics, my team of students came upon a three-year-old boy whose body position alone suggested that he had acute bacterial meningitis. He lay on his back. But his muscles were rigid: only his heels and the back of his head touched the sheets. His back was arched in a grizzly backward C. The arching was caused by inflammation of the meningeal layer, the arachnoid that was irritated by the inflammatory process.

We needed to sample his spinal fluid to isolate the offending organism, but the iron-stiff arch in his lower spine made it impossible to put a needle into his spinal canal and retrieve the cerebrospinal fluid that was needed to direct our therapy. The vertebrae would have to be separated by arching his spine in the opposite direction to allow passage of a needle into the water-filled space around the spinal cord.

I had read about another method of obtaining spinal fluid by inserting a needle into the back of the neck just below the first vertebra in the neck. It was called a cisternal tap, which I had neither seen nor done myself. I asked the residents, and they vaguely recalled its name but knew nothing more.

We laid the toddler on his stomach, cleansed the area just below the back of his head, and injected a drop of Xylocaine(TM) anesthetic under the skin. I began to push a spinal needle into his neck. I proceeded very slowly, checking the needle for fluid. The child's breathing had been deep and rapid, alternating with periods of apnea—no breathing at all. This was a sign that his brain stem, where the body's breathing center resides, was involved by his infection. I moved the needle forward just another millimeter or so. The kid suddenly stopped breathing! I pulled the needle back just a touch, and he breathed again. And cloudy fluid began flowing through the hollow needle.

I collected the spinal fluid sample and rushed to the lab, where I stained a smear made from the fluid on a glass slide, a three-minute procedure. Under the microscope, the fluid contained white blood cells and numerous dark-blue dots, stuck together in pairs. The kid had pneumococcal meningitis. I raced back to the ward, ordered the medicine, retrieved it from the pharmacy, and personally administered the first dose of intravenous antibiotics.

The little boy survived.

And I knew that I had been close, so close, to pithing the boy like a frog. I never forgot that kid—his cries, his terror, his spine arched like some gruesome parody of normal. That child convinced me that my responsibility was to do the best I knew to do.

My head was not constantly in the clouds or a book. Anne's job and my studies could not preclude the importance of my role and my growth as husband and father.

Our second daughter, Sara, was born during my fourth year at Baylor. I still remember Anne hauling out the same maternity dress she'd worn before Martha was born. But her second pregnancy was complicated by high blood pressure and swelling in her feet and legs. I knew just enough about obstetrics to be silently terrified about a disorder called preeclampsia. Undaunted, Anne worked as programmer, wife, mother, chief bottle washer, and mistress of the house.

I still remember Sara's birth. Unlike her sister, this child was lovely the moment her head emerged from her mother's womb. As Anne was taken from the delivery room, she wept briefly.

"I'm sorry it wasn't a boy."

"Not to worry, my dearest. It was my sperm's fault. It wasn't your doing"

I rejoiced in every extra minute I had to spend with my growing family. As she had done after Martha's birth, Anne returned to work within weeks after Sara was born. And it was our great fortune to bring Odessa out of retirement to provide the same affection and care to our second daughter.

During my fourth year, plastic surgery was the surgical specialty most exciting to me. I loved making scars disappear and tissue planes look full and normal. Every week we traveled to the state prison in Huntsville, Texas, where an endless line of men and women wanted their noses straightened, tattoos removed—anything to make them less recognizable than in their present state. There was too much work for our supervising resident, but there was a scrub nurse, an inmate, who could foresee virtually every potential problem and could take an attentive surgery student through any plastic surgical or orbital repair procedures. Repairing orbital fractures became my specialty. A blow to the cheekbone or the nose often fractured one or more bones of the orbit of the eye. Untreated, the eyes remained misaligned, and the patient was doomed to double vision for life. Reduction of the fracture involved repair of the orbital floor (the top wall of the sinus behind the cheekbone), application of some fine wire, and careful suturing of the tissue around the eyeball and the delicate skin above and below the eye—and voila! I loved it!

"She's terrific!" I exclaimed during a break. "Why is someone that good in here?"

"Killed her husband with an ax."

As much as I loved plastic surgery, I learned that at Baylor, a plastics fellowship came after four years of general surgery residency. At Ben Taub, that meant operating every other day (and night) for four years. I was beginning to get shooting pains down the backs of my legs after long periods of standing. It was worse if I leaned backward, pulling on a wound spreader to improve the surgeon's field of vision in an operative bed. I didn't know why it was there. It just was, and I had to deal with it.

I *knew* I didn't have the physical stamina to endure that pain for four years. Was there any program of merit that could have been less demanding? I didn't have the slightest idea. A physically less demanding residency, or the possibility of a corrective solution for the cause of my pain, simply never entered my head. I knew only that physically I could not survive four years on my feet.

As the year wound down, I needed to select my internship, or rather, wait for a hospital to select me from among the hordes of applicants. Anne wanted to return to the East for a time. In my head, there were only a few choices: Harvard and Massachusetts General Hospital (MGH), Yale–New Haven Hospital, and Johns Hopkins in Baltimore. My tickets were good. I could go pretty much anywhere I wanted. The old insecurities came back to nibble at the base of my brain. I did not relish bashing heads with the arrogant at the MGH. Baltimore, I had heard, was not a place for young children. That left Yale–New Haven Hospital. Dr. Lang, my mentor in oncology begged me stay in Houston, but there were no rewards attached or even suggested. He wanted me to join his group after completion of my training. I was flattered beyond words. But his was no longer the only such overture in town.

I had to test my mettle against the best of them. I promised to return, but I was New Haven bound.

At med school graduation, I returned to the podium time after time to receive a prize or monetary award. My daughters squealed with glee and jumped on their seats, their morning-manufactured curls bouncing like gleaming, soft springs.

I was full of myself, delighted to win the awards. In my heart, I wanted to show Dr. DeBakey that he had been wrong.

He was not present at the ceremony.

I'd traveled my own path from a point of sheer terror to stand at the top of my class with both an MD and a master's degree. Baylor was as proud of me as I was of my family and myself.

But then it was time for reality to bite.

At the close of the ceremony, Leo presented me with my unpaid college loans from Harvard. He had been able to contribute not one penny.

Anne and I were already in debt to our eyeballs with medical school bills. As an intern, I would make an astonishing $3,000 a year. Our only path to breaking even would be one baby step after another. And like most young couples, every time we saved a few hundred dollars, the toilet got plugged, or a pet had to be put to sleep. It seemed that the climb to security was impossibly long and hard.

As my mother and father joined our little clan, I saw the old, uncomfortable, all-too-familiar isolation in my parents' faces. Leo remarked that he had never seen a postgraduate ceremony before. That was it.

My mother, poor woman, was all smiles. But her head was empty of anything but her hatred for her husband.

But in the face of all the pathos and futility I saw in my parents, I felt tremendous freedom! I had taken *my* path, done it *my* way—with my wife's bloody good common sense and council and affection. I had my own clan and would nurture them, as my parents had not done.

Money, past and future, had never concerned me. During medical school, Anne and I had enough to feed ourselves, and later to clothe our kids. But the costs of medical school left us deeply in debt despite Anne's well-paying job as a programmer for a company called Shell Development. Later, she went to work at M.D. Anderson designing, monitoring, and packaging the data from research protocols. I contributed what I could, with moonlighting, and lab-managing all-nighters, and the modest stipend I got for teaching gross anatomy and histology to the incoming students. How my wife kept us all together during those years amazes me even now.

CHAPTER TWELVE

The move to New Haven was eminently forgettable. Now we had two bored, bright, feisty young children with us. ("This is my side of the line! You can't sit on my side!") We had possessions, which we packed in a U-Haul truck. My only vivid memory of the journey was cresting a hill in Tennessee and watching helplessly as the truck's back end tried to pass its front end.

Ultimately, we arrived at my parents' home in Norwalk, where we stayed while house hunting in New Haven. We found a small condominium in Hamden that almost fit our budget. The hospital was a short two miles away.

After we were settled in, we made the short trip from New Haven to Twelve Homer Street.

We had been invited to dinner and arrived as requested. Esther greeted us, exclaiming, "Oh! What a nice surprise!"

There was no dinner. She had no recollection of her invitation. Instead, we ordered a takeout meal and brought dinner to her. Leo's behavior, apart from a warm, grandfatherly embrace for the girls, was the same. He collected his meal, and when the niceties were done, he retired to his study. He was invariably asleep by the time we left to return home.

During our infrequent, Martha and Sara searched for hidden treasures. They called us to see a freezer stuffed to overflowing with dozens of packages of identical frozen TV dinners. Grandmother's closet was remarkable for at least a dozen boxes of identical pairs of shoes.

Strangely, it had the ring of my experience long ago in a similar closet.

One day, Leo called Anne. He howled his frustration that Esther habitually got herself lost on the way home while doing routine errands in Norwalk. He was flummoxed: What to do? Debbie, who was not married at this time, lived at home but had no vehicle to retrieve her mother. It had not occurred to her to call a friend or a taxi. We were deeply concerned.

Over the next two years, I spent most of my free hours falling asleep with my face in my dinner plate. But Leo faced a series of crises he was not prepared to handle. What would happen to Debbie? She had no friends, no future, and no career. What was wrong with Esther? She did not have the family disease, of course. But what could he do? At Anne's suggestion, Leo took her to see at least two specialists in New York City. Her behavior during each examination confounded Leo. She was attentive, appropriate, and cogent. She confabulated brilliantly to explain the issues of her apparent misdirection.

Esther was pronounced "normal." She used her clean bill of health as a tool to berate her husband and to defiantly assure Anne and me that Leo was the sick one in the house. And her pronouncements were laced with malevolence.

I had more important issues at hand. Yale was to be the crucible of my training. I had chosen this training program in part because it still had an every other night call schedule. There were few of those left in the United States, even by 1971. But I was (and am) convinced this stage of my apprentice training was best endured rather than enjoyed. It was performance under fire, and it required the best I had in me to give. At its most demanding, I went to work on Friday morning and returned home Monday night, usually with minimal sleep. That marathon was repeated every two weeks. (You have seen a sample in Chapter One.)

There were at least a few others who agreed with me. My fellow interns were largely easterners, my once-presumed regional nemeses. But they were bright, ingenious, and skilled physicians. I learned more from them over the next two years than I did from any academic icon.

To my surprise, I could hold my own with them. In many ways, I was more aggressive and assertive than they.

But I had major problems with senior staff members. They were often too conservative and mousy for me. I was caring for the patient. I did what was needed quickly and confidently, and I dealt with the results. But too often I was chided or criticized for my actions.

The following year, as a second-year resident, I was a tough taskmaster with medical students and new interns. I continued to insist that every second or minute saved could mean a life.

"If you needed data, get it, *now*. Don't wait for the transport guy. Wheel your patient to be scanned or whatever *yourself*. You'll learn from your patients while they're in a different setting. Talk to 'em as you walk. Prove your concern by your actions.

"If you can't get data the usual way, figure a way to get comparable or even more valuable information. Do it yourself, or at least carefully review all the information available. See every X-ray as it's being done, if you can. Hover over the lab people. They're often flattered to know clinical information from you that may avert a crisis or save a life."

I was a harsh critic when it came to reviewing students' histories and physical examinations. All the minutia I'd learned early in med school became dramatically offered pearls, which I would drop at their feet to increase their awareness and to have some gentle fun at their expense.

The medical students and interns didn't soon forget me or what I was trying to impress upon them. Whether they chose to approach patients differently or not was not my affair.

Nonetheless, I'd had enough of New Haven. I called the chief of medicine at Houston's Methodist Hospital in the Texas Medical Center.

"Hi. This is Peter Kennedy. Do you need another resident for next year?"

"Why, hello, Peter. Good to hear from you. In fact, we need a chief resident. And I'm going to be gone a fair amount. President of the American College of Cardiology, you know. So you'll have some extra duties. Can I count on you?"

"I'll be there."

Just like that, I was leaping from one lion's den into another. But it was a lion's den I knew!

CHAPTER THIRTEEN

Undoubtedly, my wife had the toughest job of all while I was out trying to find my place in the world. I made precious little money as a house officer—my resident's pay in Houston was $4,500 a year. So at each new venue, she had to find a new job, get day care for the girls, enroll them in new schools, figure a way to spread our ancient furniture about the house, and develop new schedules, rules, and boundaries.

Meanwhile, I was out the door, going lickety-split, doing the things that consumed my life. Despite my limited time with Sara and Martha, I was a pretty good dad. I didn't see them play baseball or swim, but they came first when they needed comforting, or scolding, or help with homework. I didn't coach their little league (although I did coach pee-wee hockey for a while in New Haven). The fact that they turned out so well is far more a tribute to their mother's upbringing and her genes than anything I offered, except maybe a little grit.

To be sure, I did plenty of my agonizing and breast beating in Anne's presence. She was *critical* to the choices I made—her organized approach and attention to detail often made her input paramount. Simply put, I ranted about my frustrations. She told me whether I was being stupid or not. And I learned to listen. Always.

She supported the move back to Houston. Climbing Yale's academic ladder was as frustrating for her as it was for me.

So we loaded everything up (we still used the $125 couch I'd bought in Cambridge), talked carefully to the girls, and pulled out of New England, with its towns upon towns. We headed back to the big sky of Texas.

When we arrived, I was immediately more comfortable. The new young house staff seemed brighter, and they were more eager for responsibility. Most of all, I was home. I recalled the "calf" lab and our platelet research, and biochemistry and rat experiments in detail as I walked the grounds.

I began my job as chief resident at the Houston Methodist Hospital. I was a tough, demanding boss. I worked with the nursing staff to improve the transparency of their interactions with interns and residents, and I demanded no less from the house staff. We developed a pretty well-oiled system.

The unexpected kicker came when Dr. McIntosh, the medicine department chair, gave me the added job of rounding in his stead with the hospital's cardiologists and cardiac surgeons. That meant spending time with the man I'd loved to hate when I was a med student.

I had been wrong.

I saw this impossibly powerful, stoop-shouldered man with burning dark eyes set deep in his face, the beaked nose, and the funny New Orleans lilt to his subtle Lebanese accent in a new light. His commitment, and his impact upon his institution and on the arena of cardiovascular surgery, had been incalculable. I learned during my tenure that he transported poor Lebanese children to Houston to repair their congenital heart diseases at no charge. He had a great number of patients from the Middle East. One could see their flowing gowns, burkas, and covered faces as they floated through the hospital.

As I completed my residency, I prepared for my two-year fellowship with Dr. Lang. As I had anticipated, I would take charge of patient care at the Ben Taub. There, the poor and sick waited in long lines to be seen. The air was sour with their sweat. Nurses labored long and hard at my side to provide the things we needed to administer chemotherapy, discuss treatment options, and provide comfort as best we could.

The work was long, and rarely exciting. On those occasions where I couldn't quite understand a patient's difficulties with immediate family or home issues, I ventured into the Fifth Ward (Houston's ghetto district) to visit patients at night in their homes. It was plain stupid to go alone. I had seen hundreds of the wounded from that region, more than enough to make me wary, but I was never approached or threatened on those visits. It was at those times that the total impact of a patient's journey to improvement or death upon his family became reality to me. In those days, there were few chemotherapy drugs. Our success rates were low. As I came to understand, providing comfort to the dying was my most important job.

As I talked with patient and family, I began to use the information I'd learned as a first- and second-year student—from a time when I had understood little or nothing about the personal and familial ravages of malignant disease. But now, as I addressed my little audiences, I felt something in the room change. And as I explained a mother's medical status, her husband, her children, and any extended family present would calm down...and give me all their attention. Some of the free-floating anxiety, and the suspicion and wariness about a physician in their home at nine p.m. began to dissipate.

I pushed past my own hesitation a little further. Patient and family were presented with a gentle reboot of sorts, a statement of data rather than information mixed with hysteria or bias. It was easier—and certainly more honest—to deal in facts rather than to make things up. Patients and their loved ones became active participants in their own disease and its treatment. I was essentially saying:

"Hold it! Stop the merry-go-round of fear and terror. Please be calm as you can for a second and listen. I will explain as simply and as completely as you need. I'll start with simple biology and anatomy. I *promise* you will understand the threat to your loved one better when I'm through."

"There will be no bullshit. You *must* know about the tumor, what it threatens to do, what it can and will do, and how it will impact life expectancy, the quality of life, and the probable course of death when it comes."

"When I am sure you understand all this, and you must try hard to do so, we'll talk about what can be done to reverse, stop, or cure this cancer. I'll tell you about treatment, warts and all. Nothing will be held back."

"Then we'll use this information to decide what we as a team think is best. If you want more information, by all means get it. If you want another opinion, I'll give you suggestions of people I think are the best. But when we're through, you should understand your loved one and your options. If you do not understand, ask. We'll do it again. This is too important for you to accept my request just because it's my request."

It took years to refine these presentations, particularly when they involved the stark visage of suffering or death. But as I became more deeply involved in it, I began to impart a quality I did not know I had—true empathy.

As I repeated this reboot process again and again, it became clear that when presented with the diagnosis of cancer, everybody, myself included, reacts the same way, "Oh my God, I'm going to die!" And quickly, our second thought is, "First I'm going to suffer, and *then* I'm going to die!" Part of my responsibility was to allay those fears.

I had been trained originally to use evasion and misdirection as tools to maintain hope. But I found all too quickly that patients and families picked up on inconsistencies--not in data presentation but in the nuances of communication. A movement of one's hands or changes in voice inflection was sometimes a tipoff to the possibility that their doctor wasn't being straight with them.

I changed my venue to the clinic examination rooms. I drew simple diagrams on exam room cover sheets, the ones that nurse threw away after each patient sat or lay on them. I began to demand that family members join the little audience. The process sometimes took an hour or more for a patient who had been allotted thirty minutes. As a result, I was always late to everything. When I was dangerously late, my staff would place themselves strategically in the office, making sure I had my slides or notes and that I knew *for sure* where I was to go and how I was going to get there.

At home, I was still an obsessive reader. My bookshelf swelled with new volumes and piles of my journal subscriptions. I voraciously engulfed all the medical data I could find. I relished conversing confidently with cardiologists, intensivists, pulmonologists, plastic surgeons, and nephrologists. Each conversation became a chance to increase my knowledge.

I began to recognize that for me, oncology was a field demanding competence in many areas of internal medicine and surgery. I was confident in my skills, and I didn't choose to relinquish them—ever!

As my three-year stay in Houston wound down, I was pressured to join the academic staff at two cancer centers, both in the Texas Medical Center. The first was with my former mentor, who had become a good friend. From him, I was given a vague promise of partnership with him at some future date, but with the immediate task of continuing my work at the general hospital. The other was Eric Fernstrom, chair of something called developmental therapeutics at M.D. Anderson. Sadly, the two *hated* each other, and my decision, whatever it was to be, would win me the eternal enmity of the other.

Fortunately for me, I had time to sort that problem out: I still had two years to give the US Army.

CHAPTER FOURTEEN

During the early days of the war in Vietnam, doctors to care for combatants were in short supply. But many young physicians were reluctant to delay critically important medical training in exchange for serving in the armed forces. The government introduced the Berry Plan, which allowed a doctor-in-training the opportunity to complete their formal medical education in exchange for two years' service in a branch of the military. The alternative was to go to the NIH and work in research. These options were presented to us in the spring of our third year in med school. Before me, I saw myself filling out a twenty-page application for the National Institutes of Health in Bethesda, Maryland, or a one-half-page form for the armed forces. It was one of the few times in my life that I'd chosen the softer, easier path, but that was exactly what I did.

I enlisted in the US Army Medical Corps as a first lieutenant in the Inactive Reserves. Without some kind of deferment, interns were stacked and shipped to Vietnam to care for wounded soldiers, squirming helplessly like impaled bugs. As a Berry planner, I had no meetings to attend, no rifle to carry. I was to receive no periodic military training. But they had me. That was in 1969.

By 1976 I had completed my fellowship and was visited by Lieutenant Colonel Joseph McCracken, a red-faced, jovial fellow who stretched the buttons of the lower half of his shirt. He came to me in his uniform, cap and all, to inform me I'd be going to Brooke Army Medical Center (BAMC) as his assistant chair. I would enter the active armed forces as what was called "an instant major."

We prepared to move again, this time from Houston to San Antonio.

Happily, the army moved us, and we were allowed to live off the base, which was a huge, sprawling complex with its own golf course for retirees. Anne once again scouted ahead and found us a single-family home with a backyard large enough for our kids and our aging Labrador retriever. It was located at the back of cul-de-sac and out of the main flow of cars, trucks, and possibly tanks. The kids were placed in school, again, and had adjustment problems, again. Anne set up her home, again, and found a supervisory position in computer programming, again. I put on my new uniform and trundled off to do whatever I was called upon to do.

Upon my arrival at Brooke Army Medical Center, my fellow conscripted physicians and I had to endure a sort of abbreviated basic training course. We fired rifles and handguns, climbed over walls, got locked in a room with some kind of toxic gas, rappelled, ran an obstacle course, and simulated a parachute jump. We faced an ordeal under fire. Tracers were fired at five feet above ground level while we crawled on our bellies through an obstacle course. The "real" basic trainees did the same course, but their bullets were fired at a three-foot level. Despite the Army's efforts to protect its new physicians, one poor young fellow from Michigan, who'd never seen a poisonous snake, came across a small rattler in his path. He panicked and stood up.

Physicians were thereafter recused from that exercise.

Initially, my work was primarily teaching the medical students, house officers, and fellows who were assigned to Brooke. They were basically a bright bunch. One of my fellows was so good I was willing to give an arm and two future draft choices if he'd join me after the army, but he preferred to remain where he was, bless him.

After a while, I got bored. The monotony was occasionally broken by occasional visits to places like Fort Polk, which we reached via an ancient, single-engine army plane. Our charge was to treat mostly retired and civilian personnel afflicted by malignant disease.

Fearsome flights notwithstanding, I wasn't content to teach for my eight hours a day. I sought out the commanding colonel of the base and discussed my earlier platelet research with him. He was intrigued and then excited. He made funds available so that I could obtain any equipment I needed to expand my work without a blink or a raised eyebrow.

I decided to try my hand at clinical trials. My only previous experience had been as a medical student. I had presented a paper at the national meeting for medical oncologists.

The original idea, as had usually been the case with me, was founded in a clinical problem that needed solving. I had treated a patient with a liver tumor, called hepatoma. This particular fellow often had episodes of profound hypoglycemia (low blood sugar) because his tumor produced excessive amounts of the blood sugar lowering hormone, insulin. He repeatedly showed up in the Ben Taub ER semiconscious, confused, and combative. A quick check of his blood glucose indicated that it was dangerously low. He recovered promptly after an intravenous injection of a glucose solution. However, these life saving injections had destroyed all his peripheral veins.. When I was called to see him, it seemed the only way to give him chemotherapy was by mouth. I had passed a small rubber tube through his nose to the back of his throat and down into his stomach. Incredibly, hours after the first treatment, he awoke and asked us what all the fuss was about!

The idea of orally administered chemotherapy was not new at that time, but it had not been used in liver cancer. So over the next year I had identified ten patients who were similarly afflicted and treated them with chemotherapy given orally. Five of them got better. Their symptoms improved, and their tumors shrank.

My mentor said, "Terrific! Write it up. You can present it."

I did, and I did. But it was not well received. In fact, I was the butt of jokes for days afterward, from the giants in oncology, no less.

I was angry, but I was mostly confused. Why would anyone present information that was not factual? If something was not worthy of further study, why lie about it?

Thus armed with the sting of prior rebuke, I chose to design a protocol that would attempt to standardize diagnosis and treatment of cancer of unknown origin. These were tumors whose organ or site of origin could not be identified. Typically, patients with this malignancy had widespread metastases present at diagnosis, did not respond to chemotherapy, and were doomed to an early death. I developed a chemotherapy regimen, which in a small pilot study we did at Brooke successfully produced tumor shrinkage in about half of the treated patients. Those patients whose tumors got smaller lived significantly longer than the rest.

The protocol was accepted for widespread distribution and patient accrual by SWOG, one of the country's four main protocol-generating agencies at the time. As I monitored the entries onto the protocol, and the data that investigators forwarded to me, I was astounded that interpretation of the information sent to me from around the country was mostly garbage. The forms were often unreadable. There were untold deviations—which I had prohibited—from the diagnostic and therapeutic interventions proscribed. How could anyone make sense of this? I left the protocol, and the data, when I left the army. I could not analyze, and draw conclusions, from information that was unreadable, imprecise, uninterpretable. I was not surprised when I noted some years later that some young Turk had parlayed my data into a published, peer reviewed publication. I was listed among the authors. But I had learned a sobering lesson. I got on with the business of starting a life.

My life as Major Kennedy ended quietly. BAMC offered me a promotion to colonel and directorship of its research center, the Byrne Unit. It would have been fine with me, but my wife and kids said, "NO!"

They'd had enough of San Antonio. It was a done deal.

Years later, while in private practice, I had two experiences that added to my skepticism regarding investigation in clinical research. In about 1979, I tried to create a network of community oncologists, which would give them the opportunity to participate in uncomplicated clinical trials. We had all been trained to participate and even to create such trials as trainees during our fellowships.

Perhaps more important, NIH grants were training a passel of us young oncologists. Academic institutions, once the haughty centers for such research, were losing trial-eligible patients to the very people they had trained. Further, the professors in medical oncology, and even their department chairs, often used these trials to garner grant money, paid speaking tours, and, of course, prowess as national leaders in their respective fields. But there were no patients! They were being treated, quite competently, by the oncologists the professors themselves had trained and released into the world.

This network was our chance to push back the frontier of clinical oncology, to add our patients, their clinical data, their long-term survival rates, and the like. This was part of what we had all been trained to do.

I presented my argument to my assembled colleagues from all over Los Angeles more than once. Their reluctance to proceed in this pioneering effort was simple. The work required for data collection and review, identification, and lengthy explanations to prospective patients all required *time*. And time meant hours spent away from one's usual duties.

"If we're paid for the time our nurses and staff have to spend away from their duties, we'll be happy to help you."

Alas, I had no money to give them. The project went *splat*.

It was about this time that the pharmaceutical industry began to investigate the same concept—but its leaders had the money. Oodles of it. Ultimately, their participation in clinical trials would change the face of oncology forever.

My hunger for pursing new ideas, which seemed to pop into my head in an instant, remained unabated. I was treating a patient with a particular kind of cancer (carcinoid tumor), often associated with severe diarrhea. Following his chemotherapy, the man returned to me, at my direction, because of uncontrollable diarrhea. But his symptoms were due to my treatment, not his tumor. I gave him a newly approved drug, Sandostatin, developed to control diarrhea caused by carcinoid tumors. I had nothing else to offer him, except seven to ten days of hospitalization and intravenous fluids, and a significant risk of death. Nothing else was effective to correct the damage caused by the chemotherapy. The patient was admitted to the hospital for appropriate supportive care. But his diarrhea was gone!!!

I called the company that made the drug, and announced my finding. They encouraged me to try it again! They sent me a small supply of Sandostatin, and I proceeded to gather a small group of patients who had received chemotherapy and now had severe diarrhea. I studied the patients six ways to Sunday. And I presented my findings at the annual meeting of oncologists from around the world. I was applauded. I was feted. During the months that followed, I gave lectures in a dizzying array of institutions. It was my fifteen minutes of fame.

But I didn't like it much. I missed my wife, my patients, and my kids. I did not enjoy eating rubber chicken and staying in a motley array of motels while I prepared to recite my findings again and again.

And when I returned from one of these junkets, I found that my treatment had been incorporated into a clinical protocol, written by a professor at one of the academic centers in LA, without obtaining my permission. In fact, my work was not even recognized among the references listed in the protocol.

Ahh. The joys of academia! I was pleased at the ready acceptance of my new treatment, but I would have enjoyed at least a hand wave. To add insult to injury, I was a Clinical Assistant Professor at that institution!

During these shenanigans, I had a second idea, which excited me even more! I heard a presentation regarding the use of tiny doses of Sandostatin ™ (a look alike cousin of somatostatin, a unique multifunctional hormone in the gut) to relieve gastric atony in diabetic patients. Atony means without muscle tone. Some diabetics' stomachs never emptied their contents; people so afflicted ate breakfast well, but were not hungry for the remainder of the day. As a consequence, they lost weight and muscle mass, and their strength deteriorated.

I thought, "What patients do I have who have gastric atony? Why, *all* of them!" My patients characteristically ate a relatively normal breakfast, but were unwilling or unable to eat again for the rest of the day. Just like diabetics with gastric atony!

What was there to lose? I designed and carried out a small study to test my hypothesis (i.e., the gleam in my eye). And it worked—again! They were hungry! Advanced, inoperable cancer patients, most receiving chemotherapy, got an itty-bitty injection of Sandostatin. Within days, over 80 percent felt well and left their beds. They gained weight and strength. It didn't seem to matter whether their cancer was responding to treatment or not. And because they were stronger and ate better, *they lived longer.*

I thought, "This is a subject that needs much more study! I need to tell someone about this!"

I wrote the paper and sent it to medical journal after medical journal. It was repeatedly rejected. I even sent it to the drug's manufacturer to review and edit. I sent it to journals as a brief communication or a letter to the editor, although it did represent my original research.

No takers. I still have the manuscript in a drawer somewhere. My hypothesis, methods, results, and conclusions were sound. I used the drug in my own patients for decades with absolutely consistent results. Why not introduce the concept to further study? I never understood.

I retreated to my golf game and my patients, and let the bright-ideas department slide. I'd seen enough of cancer research to scare hell out of me.

CHAPTER FIFTEEN

As my assignment at BAMC came to a close, it was time to decide what I was going to do (I thought) for the rest of my life.

After all those years of excitement and adventure, it was time to grow up. Time to find a job. Time to take all my excitement, my experience, and my family on the road to join the big show.

I prepared a detailed curriculum vitae (which I haven't looked at in thirty-plus years). I'd written a passel of scientific of papers. Since most of them involved basic or clinical research, and I loved teaching, it seemed logical to seek an academic position. I hoped I could find a med school that would be interested in the type of work I'd done.

At Baylor I'd combined my patient care experience with every opportunity to be involved in research at everything from cell morphology and lipid research to clinical trials. I had devised and experimentally validated out a biochemical trick to identify the active site of an enzyme essential to mammalian metabolism (fumarase). We were among the first to investigate the deposition of nonmetabolized lipid deposits (from vegetable oils) among patients with atherosclerotic vascular (blood vessel) disease. We got the arteries within moments after they were removed from patients requiring vessel replacement by Dr. DeBakey, my one-time object of scorn.

I became close friends with a pulmonary department clinical professor whose interest was in the physiology of platelet aggregation. The lab itself was directly above Dr. DeBakey's operating suite. In my spare time, and at night, I helped work on development of the cardiotomy sump filter, the device that is now routinely used in all open-heart operations to return one's own blood safely to the circulation, reducing the need for a blood transfusion during open-heart surgery. I'd helped to develop and test the first in-line blood filters that removed clot and debris from stored blood before it was infused into the body, a particular hazard to patients in septic shock or in respiratory failure. I developed an assay to quantitatively measure platelet function in patients whose platelet counts were too low to be measured using existing methods. I'd seen platelet function abnormalities rarely, if ever, described in the literature, like the poor man who developed a "stone heart" (a heart that stops, and dies, during a prolonged contracted state, empty of blood). His vessels were filled with "casts" of platelets that mirrored the vessels' interior perfectly.

We had worked on a left ventricular assist device (LVAD), one of the first devices known as the artificial heart. It was then a huge apparatus driven by a compressed oxygen-nitrogen-CO_2 mixture that was connected to the animals' hearts by tubes as large as a fist. The devices were large and stationary. So were the animals. But occasionally, one would develop labored breathing or fall to its knees. I carried a special beeper on my hip to alert me if one of the cows in the "calf lab" became ill. If I ever heard the alert "Code Blue. Clarabelle Vaca," I ran like hell to save the calf. It seemed like an open door for further exploration. It surely was! But that is another story.

At Yale, my enthusiasm was also contagious. Fellow interns gave me a blood-stained harpoon as a recognition my aggressiveness. I tagged along with the first US physician to do research in acupuncture. (He was the only guy in the medical center who read Chinese.) The cardiology department head invited me to join that team as a staff member specializing in emergency pacemaker placement and EKG research.

Teaching had always been a kick. There had been lectures presented to students, physicians, and large gatherings of academicians during my training. When decorum allowed, I'd intersperse ridiculous, irrelevant slides among dry graphs and charts to get a laugh, and I would often plant wrong answers with members of the audience and then get overly dramatic in my criticism of the "offender." After all, keeping eighty-five to two hundred doctors awake and interested, especially if they'd just finished lunch and were sitting in a darkened hall for sixty minutes, was no mean feat.

But all that took a backseat now. I phoned contacts, wrote letters, and cornered department heads at meetings. My first options included M.D. Anderson, Baylor College of Medicine, Yale, and the army.

But they each represented problems:

1. My kids and Anne hated San Antonio, at least the army part. The city was populated primarily by retired military personnel, so there were few kids to play with. There was a new medical school starting in San Antonio that offered me a position, but the family had said, "Nix!" The army, too, was out, despite the prospect of shiny silver bird on my collar and a whole research department to manage.
2. In Houston, my former chief had always felt that I would return and work for him. My job was to be operation of the oncology division at the Ben Taub Hospital. However, my opportunity to see private patients and develop a referral base of my own seemed to represent a threat of some sort. What would be open for me in the future? Anne, Martha, and Sara had followed me from job to job without complaint. But they had done without material things for a long time. I had presented Anne with all the jeweled finery I could afford while we were in college, but there was no money for it now. My most lavish gift to myself had been a thirty-dollar battery for my $200 Nash Rambler.
3. The alternative in Houston was to join the staff at M.D. Anderson. The chair there, Dr. Eric Fernstrom,, was excited about the prospect of having a platelet specialist on his staff; my research in platelet function filled his bill. As I have noted, my problem was that the heads of oncology at Baylor and M.D. Anderson hated each other. My selection of one

program over another would be akin to offering my head on a plate so that one giant in oncology could taunt the other with my bloody remains.
4. Also, base salary at the University of Texas hospital system was pretty skimpy. It wasn't much better at Baylor, for that matter. And it would take two to four years for me to establish myself, carve out my teaching responsibilities, and begin to seek grant support for me, my lab, my staff, and, of course, for the medical school that hired me.
5. We (mostly I) hadn't been happy in New Haven. There was work for Anne, but getting the girls into a good school would be time consuming and uncertain. Mostly, I had resigned and flown the coop before my assignment as chief resident was over because I felt stifled by what I perceived as the provincialism of the academicians in charge of the program. That had been the reason I'd returned to Houston in the first place! I thought I knew the Harvard way, and I *surely* knew the Yale way. Since all other centers in the East wanted in their heart of hearts to emulate those two, I was reluctant to fool with them.

I had to skip town. But there were surprisingly few positions available around the country. Everyone seemed to have a junior trainee who could slide into the position of assistant professor without ruffling a feather. I was still puffed up and full of myself, so I squawked and hollered and waved my arms. "I'm here! I'm terrific! You *need* me!"

There were a few bites. The chair of the program at the University of Arkansas needed a new man with new ideas.

That was me! But Arkansas? I was intrigued, but I was *always* intrigued. Anne said, "I don't think so!" As always, she was probably right.

The West Coast had always been scary to us. We had decided that LA and San Francisco were danger zones. Our kids would get hooked on drugs. Worse, we'd get pressured into some wild partner swap—all unthinkable! It was not an option. Oregon and Washington? All we knew was that it rained too much.

But I'd received two warm invitations from LA—one from City of Hope and one from the University of Southern California Medical School. So I flew to Los Angeles, stayed in a hotel that sat just behind a racetrack near a town called Arcadia, and was transported by limousine to the ER at USC.

Upon entering the emergency room, I saw lines of red blanket-covered gurneys and endless lines of sick people waiting for attention.

My brain yelled, "What the hell? I just *left* this place! This is another Ben Taub!"

So I tried the second Southern California opportunity, City of Hope. There a small man with a few hairs pasted across his scalp escorted me to an office where multiple copies of a single paper adorned all four walls. His name was Dr. Maurice Opfer, and he had discovered a rare variant of malignant lymphoma, cancer of the lymph nodes.

Once introduced, he showed me his domain. We walked from his office to the ward, a distance of some twenty feet. There were five inpatient beds available for treatment of the sick and dying.

I was shocked. It was routine for me to manage thirty to thirty-five hospitalized patients at a time, plus outpatients and research.

"I've been used to a pretty large patient load. I've always accepted any patient who came through the door."

"It's not a problem. You'll get over it," he said. "You will pick a tumor type, like I did, and make a name for yourself! That's how you make your mark in cancer research."

That was unacceptable. I'd succeeded by my passion to know and understand *everything*, only to be told that *real* success was to be earned by letting it sit, like compost, in my head.

Depression, confusion, and frustration rolled over me like a wave. I saw my future as an administrator, vying for control of more bed space and cleverly slitting the throats of my departmental colleagues (whom I would recruit so we could plot against and replace the small, bald fellow).

City of Hope had originally been a sanatorium for patients with tuberculosis, and the pulmonary physicians held their territory as if it were fields of gold! We would fight the lung doctors and their colleagues for political clout to get the facilities we needed. We'd have to conspire with their foes to amass power in the form of grant money and gifts dedicated to the medical center. I'd spend my productive years playing political games to achieve goals of control and program direction. It was not in me to do that sort of stuff! I knew it. My choice of battlefield had been the bedside. That was where time stopped for me. That was where I was truly happy.

Over many years, I have concluded that was where I was as close to God as I could get. During my years in medicine, what I'd loved and lived for had been learning and processing new information, pursuing new ideas that popped into my head from nowhere, sharing what I'd come to understood with colleagues, and using the data to care for the sick and dying in my charge.

I spent the early hours of that night as a visiting dignitary in an unused hospital bed at the City of Hope Hospital. Drenched with my own sweat, concern, worry, and confusion enveloped me.

I had always had reservations about the unending pursuit of new grant money to support my work and my staff. Even more odious was the political and interpersonal competition that represented a huge part of that game. I had seen its effects in spades over and over again at institutions like Yale, Baylor, and Harvard.

Now, as far west as my apparent horizon could stretch, I was comfortable and confident in the skills I'd developed. But there seemed to be nobody who wanted them.

I did not have the slightest idea how to convert my aggressiveness with specific medical situations into a tool that would enable me to barge my way into fame and honor at a powerful, influential institution that didn't know me from Adam. My reputation had been made by my actions, not by the number of publications in my CV or by my academic achievements. I never had an interest in wooing departmental bigwigs. I never attended national meetings to see whom I could meet and leach from.

Like my father before me, I had neither a master plan for advancement nor any sense of how to proceed. For him, it had been book to book and then phrase to phrase, all from that incredible storehouse and his limitless imagination. For me, I guess it had been word to word and then a dim outline of a construct, and then from one exciting idea—and how to prove it—to the next. (It is ironic that after almost half a century, I still remember the precise words on the pages I used to make the body's parts an integral whole.)

Lost to me in my despair was that actions had defined me again and again at the institutions where those very traits and their truths had been demonstrated.

Then at 11:30 p.m., an angel appeared to me in the parking lot outside my temporary guest residence. He was driving a Cadillac Seville, and his name was Dr. Robert McKenna. He had heard about me from a young ex-army surgeon who was now in his employ. He was cordial, friendly, even. He apologized for the late hour.

Briefly, Dr. McKenna described that he and three other cancer surgeons had formed a cancer surgical group, which had a well-respected thirty-year history in the Los Angeles area. Over the years, they had given their own chemotherapy, but medical oncology's tools were becoming more sophisticated, and referring physicians were beginning to question the surgeons' techniques and results. Why were surgeons giving chemotherapy in the first place? Would I consider serving as their chemotherapist? I would be asked to treat patients who required systemic treatment. It would be equally important to become known among their referring physicians.

"Would I? Hell, *yes*! Where do I sign?" I said yes but didn't know Los Angeles from a fried egg. I didn't know the first thing about the geography of the region, the living costs, fires, earthquakes, or a riptide from a Rottweiler. With my usual naïveté, none of that mattered. I'd found a home where my girls would be tanned and lovely, and Anne would no longer have to support my rear end!

There was more to excite me. Dr. McKenna envisioned a Southern California network of community-based medical oncologists who could perform clinical trials and contribute in a real way to the advancement of patient well-being and survival.

The concept was an important one, although still in infancy. In the early years of cancer research, studies had been done almost exclusively at large academic teaching centers. Community practitioners were considered inferior in their ability to produce meaningful and reliable research data. But in 1975, a small trial from New England showed improved treatment results and survival among patients treated by community physicians against a specific type of acute leukemia. I'd actually discussed those results with the president of a large regional cooperative group. He'd scratched his head for a moment, stuttered a couple of questions, and then turned on his heel and stormed away.

Logically, the increased number of newly trained medical oncologists meant that more and more bright, well-prepared cancer physicians were entering the community. There was no space for them in the teaching centers where'd they trained. As these doctors opened their offices and became part of their communities, patients would come to them for treatment. As a result, fewer cancer patients would have to leave their own communities to travel to major cancer treatment centers. The centers themselves would soon have fewer patients available for protocol treatment.

For me, at this moment, this was *perfect*! Research and private practice, too! I said yes before I called Anne.

When I called her the next morning, the lady was *not* pleased. Where would we live? How would we live? What about the girls, the drugs, wife swapping, and all that?

No matter! We'd work it out!

Anne flew to LAX the next day. One of the partners greeted her and took us for a tour of Beverly Hills.

"You like that one?" he said, pointing to a palatial structure with seemingly endless acres of grounds. "Forget it. You can't afford it."

(He himself had found a small place hidden on the edge of BH.)

He was joking. But he wasn't. I had visions of my whole house of cards collapsing before it could be built. Later, he chortled, "The other partners lived on the 'east side.'"

We holed up in our Arcadia motel, miserable and angry. We had rarely fought verbally, but we were close now. This night all the marbles were on the table.

"Is this what you really want to do?" she asked.

"I wish I knew. I would give almost anything to stop this goddamn game playing. Tonight I just want you and the kids to be happy and safe, and for all of you to get the opportunities you want or need."

"The first thing you must decide is what you *really* want!"

Silence. Then, partly in jest, I said,

"Remember when I took almost the whole school year—always at night—to finish that rat experiment on pH and platelet clumping?

"I went through three hundred animals. The first twenty gave perfect results. The next two-hundred were all over the lot. Then all of a sudden, I became 'rat aorta-puncturing proficient.' Or something. I felt like I could have the model say anything I wanted it to. And I didn't know why. Finished the study in two nights, wrote it up, and published it. And now it's lost somewhere in a sea of information.

"It's a tiny island of excellence, or, at least, my best effort at it that will probably never be seen. There's important, maybe critical, information there, like the fact that platelets don't work a damn in acidotic blood, like in the patient with sepsis who bleeds and bleeds. Platelets don't work well when they're removed from whole blood in the blood bank. It may be due to the slightly acid solution all donated blood is stored in. But everybody does it! Without a peep!"

I was rambling now. But it was time to get it out. What kind of corner had I painted myself into? "What does all that mean? My model was accurate and correct. Was my method just erratic enough at first that the answer's in my hands and is otherwise irrelevant? Can't accept that. And down the line, who will consent to produce a particle counter that we first found in the basement of Walter Reed Medical Center? It was used for sizing mud particles in the oil fields! Who will support me while I work backward to re-create and someday to mass-produce a device so sensitive all blood-product transfusion will have to be reexamined? So some dude in east Nebraska can begin our work again? All credit to him! That is, *if* he has the bucks to do the work or the skill to do it right?

"One thing important I have learned. At 2:00 a.m., I'd much rather be awakened by a patient's call for help than by somebody telling me I've got to go check my rats. And, I guess, I'm learning what I'm saying now. I can't live comfortably in a world full of academic Titans, screaming and jumping up and down to be heard. I'm a sad case. Crazy to be first and best on the dance floor. Then crazy that I'm out there alone. What I'm really good at, and where I'm most comfortable, is taking care of sick folks. And teaching others how to do it."

"You choose what you really want. Then we'll be fine. I promise you."

The next morning, Dr. McKenna intervened. He had never heard a word of my desperate blabbering. But he measured men well. Except for a fancy dinner in Beverly Hills, we avoided the west side and found a small starter home, compliments of McKenna's neighbor, who had found McKenna's house for him. The home was clean and the front yard well manicured. The house had an exceptionally large backyard.

The town was called San Marino. Except for the royal palms lining its main street, it looked like any other little town. But the public schools were among the best in the state, and from our front door, the girls could walk to school. Dr. McKenna and his wife had raised their children in the system.

But there was the money. We had sold a house in Houston for a whopping $70,000. And we thought we were ready for any event. But not for LA. This teeny house, with two bedrooms, a hallway, and a glassed-in lanai, cost $230,000. Sweet Jesus!

As was always typical of me, I had no idea what my salary would be. "Don't worry," we were told. "Everything's high here. Your salary will cover it easily."

It didn't. Not even close. And thus began my life as a private practitioner in Southern California.

CHAPTER SIXTEEN

Again, just like so many times in the past, it was done. We loaded the girls into our family car and headed west from San Antonio to San Marino. Fortunately, my new colleagues paid for this move, so the mood among us Kennedy travelers was more eager and relaxed.

My own terrors were familiar ones. Would I measure up? I'd be entering hospital-associated medical staffs for the first time, a new kind of politics, new turf to compete for, and largely unknown responsibilities to fulfill. I had a head full of information and was confident in my ability to care for patients. It was the job of selling myself to an entirely unknown population of physicians that scared hell out of me.

The first night was easy. We had no furniture, so we piled into sleeping bags and slept in the living room of our new-old (circa 1928) Spanish-style stucco house with a Mexican tile roof.

Anne's labors were more pressing. She had to quiet the fears and insecurities of a nine-year-old and an eleven-year-old, set up a home, forge schedules, and find food, clothing, hardware, and shops that were convenient and reliable. If that wasn't enough, my job did not pay for mortgage, auto upkeep, insurance, etc. She had to find a job herself and deal with all the machinations that would inevitably follow our wholesale transfer to a part of the country that had scared the bejesus out of all of us.

As was her way, Anne wasted little time in setting up contacts and interviews. She was a veteran of the statistical evaluation and oversight of clinical trials. She'd been an essential force in nationally recognized results from studies done at M D Anderson Hospital, where she'd worked first as a programmer and then as a statistical analyst and supervisor. Within a year or two of her arrival in LA, she earned a master's degree in statistics from USC while keeping her position at the Children's Cancer Study Group statistical office and making her family toe the line. Later, she reinvented herself as a major force in the development of a nonprofit, totally free-of-cost support center for cancer patients and their families (The Wellness Community–Foothills).

She returned to graduate school *again* and earned an MBA from UCLA.

She emerged from this a different woman. Her chronic slouch was gone; mine has remained, alas. Her green eyes fairly sparkled and danced, expressing confidence, openness, and concern I had not seen before. She could entertain and control a roomful of wealthy donors, or form a bond with a single patient or family who were filled with fear and rage. It was beautiful to see! It has always been those green, green eyes!

Martha, our older daughter, was hard hit by the move. She was a good little athlete, a gritty gymnast, and a devotee of Martina Navratilova. But she was thrown from central Texas gymnastics into the US of A lions' den of would-be gymnastics champions. Southern California was a hotbed of lithe, tiny, slim-limbed forty-five-pound leapers, jumpers, and highfliers, all vying for regional or even national recognition.

She was overwhelmed. She'd wear her orange practice leotard until it could stand and dance on its own. She was sullen and withdrawn, and she smelled of old, stubborn sweat—a far cry from the flaxen-haired, blue-eyed, mousy kid who'd been impressive with her grit, power, and tenacity. Soon enough, she found a friend, a neighbor with similar interests and similar growing pains. And she was off to run her own race, as I would learn to my boundless astonishment, amazement, and wonder.

Over the next few years, I watched with wonder as she found her way in her new world. She forged friendships, became a swimmer of real merit, and, although always a bit reserved, found a women's college in Boston after graduation. She never once considered a future as a druggie or a dropout; she was her mother's kid.

Almost all our fears had been silly.

Almost. I literally had to beat the boys away with a stick. (One hid in the bushes beside our house for hours and surrendered his vigil only when threatened with the business end of a baseball bat.)

When she was about thirteen, Martha came to me for a serious discussion. First, she was changing her name to Elisabeth (her middle name). Martha no longer "fit" her. Second, she DID NOT WANT TO BE ANYTHING LIKE ME! That meant *no more physicians* in the family. What could I say? I guess I had not been a good role model. At least she didn't want to be a statistician either.

After high school graduation, Martha (who later changed her name formally to Elisabeth) went to the girls' college in Boston for a year and then announced that she was returning home.

She did so with a flair and incisiveness I'd not seen in her before. When she arrived, she had already been accepted at Occidental College, defined her major, and found roommates and a place to live. After graduating with a major in art history, she went to work at a local gallery. Within weeks she was selling art for the owner.

She spent one summer peering into our oven. When she was satisfied with whatever she'd been looking at, she designed and mass-produced her invention. The first baked tortilla chip. When a large baking company stole her idea, she came to work for me and learned how to run my office. After several years, she began a second company, which provided management and billing advice to medical oncologists. Her mother's kid!

Sara, our younger girl, had fewer obvious difficulties. She hooked up easily with the neighbor kids, excelled in school, and ultimately chose to attend Wellesley College as her mother had done. Like falling off a log. I entirely missed the agonies of her early adolescence. I was off in my new world, getting recognized and struggling for trust and respect.

Later, Sara was a bit subtler about rejecting the doctor's dynasty. When it was time to pick a college and a career, she chose a career in medicine because her boyfriend was going to go to medical school. When he did not get into college at all, she chose Wellesley as a second option.

Ironically, both girls, like their mother, would later be involved in cancer care in one form or another.

As for me, I started out running two feet off the ground and scared spitless. I was a researcher! A lousy professorial wannabe! I listened intently as my three employers urged me gently into my routine. My main area of practice was to be in downtown LA, the site of the group's original office. I would work five half days at our main office and see hospital inpatients when required. In addition, I was to work a half day in each of two other offices, one some thirty miles to the east in San Gabriel, and a second about twenty-five miles to the northeast in Glendora. I would be paid $500 per month for my work in the San Gabriel Valley, plus $50,000 per year for my work in Los Angeles. To me, it was a handsome sum. Anne was not so sure. This was Los Angeles, for God's sake!

I began the process of applying to the medical staffs of some sixteen hospitals that were within my zone of geographic responsibility. I thought, "Whew! At least I'll be able to feel my way into this." But there were obligatory tours of hospital facilities, interviews, meetings, conferences, and something called a "tumor board." And there were so many of them!

I determined that traffic would not be a problem if I left before the morning rush began, and then I proceeded along traffic routes against the heaviest flow to make my way to meetings and to see patients. Managing traffic was of huge importance: I saw it as the difference between helping my girls grow up, and remaining a sideline spectator, a nonparticipant, a zombie. Almost daily I was invariably asked to a see the patient who was hospitalized at the wrong end of my circuit, and who needed me at the wrong time of day. Far too often, I was stricken with what I came to call "freeway creep", instead of enjoying the open highway that went in the opposite direction.

To make matters worse, I struggled through wall-to-wall cars at mid-day as I attempted the impossible. I had been selected as Cancer Committee chair in several community hospitals simultaneously. As a consequence, it was too often my responsibility to lead two meetings, often miles apart, in a single hour. It was stupid, frustrating, maddening, infuriating. But I kept trying anyway. (After several months, committee members cheered and laughed when I arrived. Some of them have since told me, "Stupid kid. Can't be everywhere at once."

But their good humor was oblique testimony to my efforts on behalf of their hospital and their patients.

A more immediate problem was the freeway system itself. The traffic was scary and bewildering! So many cars, so close together, going so fast—or not going at all! In all directions at once! Highways merging or heading to places I'd never heard of. I was suddenly in a directional dunce. I consistently took the wrong off-ramp or merged onto a freeway going in the wrong direction, heading for a place called Santa Barbara or San Diego or Palm Springs. If GPS existed in 1978, I didn't know about it.

Once, Anne and I went to visit my maternal grandmother, who lived on Victory Boulevard in Reseda. How hard could it be? We took the Victory Blvd. exit off a freeway we knew and drove thirty-five miles due east without finding the place. Then we turned around and drove fifty miles in the other direction with the same result. Surely, there was not a fifty-mile-long city street anywhere else on the entire continent!

Fortunately, my offices were all close to a sort of closed circuit that ran from downtown LA eastward on one freeway and then circled back and returned west on a second freeway to the same downtown area. My sixteen assigned hospitals were perched like low-hanging fruit around that circuit. I could do it! All would be well: we could pay the mortgage. Our kids would not have to beg for alms.

What I did not consider was the stuff I did not yet understand, and, worse, could never control. My first introduction to community-based medical oncology came during an interview at a large downtown hospital. There, the chair of medicine—a tall, sandy-haired man with muttonchops and a huge, waxed moustache—sat me down on a footstool and berated me from behind his mahogany desk for treating cancer patients who were going to die anyway, and in short order! What good did I do for anybody? It was a year before I returned to that place. Even then, simply walking the hospital's halls gave me sweaty palms.

In fact, my own ignorance was the real cause of my awful experience. I shortly learned that essentially all community hospitals elected department chairs from among its medical staff. The winner was often as not the loser--because no one else wanted the job! On the contrary, my own experience in academics had been that a department chair was a famous person who had written lots of groundbreaking papers and controlled tons of grant money.

I clearly had a lot to learn. (I have since been a section chair, a department chair, and a chief of staff—several times, and at several hospitals where I cared for patients.!)

One hospital—now long closed—made me director of resident training. Then as a reward for my hard work (and I did work!), I was elected chief of staff, not once but twice. I now believe it was because I did not speak conversational Spanish well. The medical staff members, most of them Hispanic, could quibble, castigate, and threaten each other, knowing I had no idea what had been said. They were, for the most part, caring doctors who liked the idea of a language-ignorant prominent oncologist in their midst. Their interpersonal feuds had begun long before I arrived and would persist after I was gone.

My second rude awakening, and one that had me routinely pounding my steering wheel, was that no matter how early in the morning I began rounds—usually about 5:30 a.m.—I invariably had to see a patient twice, or see a new case, later that day. And I invariably had to struggle through the commuter jam in one or both directions before returning to my primary office to finish seeing patients.

Then there were the tumor boards. These were weekly meetings held as educational sessions for the medical staff. They were usually held at noon, and free lunch was served. The meetings served as a forum where new cancer doctors could essentially "perform" as they discussed new cases presented to them. An impressive showing usually led to more referrals, which meant more patients to treat. In addition, it was de rigueur to serve on one or two medical staff committees, which generally met once a month. But there were sixteen hospitals, all with similar meetings and different medical staffs. I frequently made an appearance at one tumor board, argued my case, and proceeded to a second conference four miles up the freeway. I bashed the wheel in not-so-silent rage. What were my limits? My real responsibilities?

During my first two years on the job, I worked sixteen to twenty hours a day. Since I was now *the* chemotherapist and couldn't have surgeons covering my chemotherapy patients, I made hospital rounds seven days a week as well. I was simply gone from my home, except between 11:00 p.m. and 5:00 a.m. There was a radio program entitled *The Radio Mystery Hour*. It ran from 10:00 to 11:00 p.m. If I arrived home before the show was over, it was a great victory!

What had happened to my job of caring for patients already established within the practice, to be transferred to my care for chemotherapy? It seemed nobody in the group worked by the same rules.

Between the two younger surgeons, one sought my assistance regularly. It was great fun to work with him! The other, who had moved his work to hospitals at the eastern periphery of my circuit, had a far smaller cadre of patients, and jealously insisted that they be treated *his* way. He had been the minority vote against hiring me.

The senior partner, Dr. McKenna, would ask me into a patient's exam room, where I would stand, hands folded in silence like a first-year medical student, while he discussed a patient who'd been cancer-free for twenty years.

The fourth surgeon, an older man who'd actually begun the practice years before, was a little batty. He saw no patients and did no surgeries. But I bet he was enjoying his comfort at the expense of my hide.

The point, I soon learned, was that there was no policy and no job description for me because none of the surgeons had the slightest idea what to do with me—or what I would do for them. What they did learn quickly was that they were making lots more money. I was, in essence, breaking new ground for them—attracting more patients and generating more income than if they all operated twenty-four hours a day, every day.

A second physician, a radiation oncologist, was brought on board about the same time I was hired. A Moroccan Jew with a French accent and a head full of tight ringlets, he was just as obsessive about delivering premium care and caring for his patients as I was!

The profits from our labors began to roll in. The surgeons were astonished! By sheer chance they'd hired two compulsive young docs who were amicable and relatively normally adjusted, and they were creating a network of referring physicians the surgeons had never dreamed of having.

On the other hand, the new radiotherapist and I were disgruntled. We were certainly making an adequate living, but where was our reward for such superlative performance and such bloody hard work?

In large measure, our dilemma was our own creation. We had both signed contracts with the following provisions:

1. Six-and-a-half years till full partnership. Why so long? "That's our decision. Take it or leave it."
2. No review of the books till you achieve full partnership. Why? "That's our decision. We think it's fair."
3. When you get to be a full partner, we split whatever profits evenly. "That's a great deal for such a large and famous practice as ours."

We were shocked. And angry. Not awed.

And also trapped. The capital costs of a radiation unit were enormous. My radiation colleague was simply neither able nor willing to work as subservient to another radiation specialist. For myself, I was still frightened about what I did not yet know about private practice of medical oncology in LA. I was *not* a businessman. I was already scared by the city. But how could I move my family again to an area where success and security would be no more certain than here?

So we hung on, grousing all the way. I hung on until first one, then another, and then another medical oncologist was hired to take over those communities where I had begun tumor boards and established specialized care units. After ten years, there were six medical oncologists doing what I had done before.

As the practice grew in numbers and influence, a second, and then a third, radiation unit was built. At peak size, there were thirteen medical oncologists, and three radiation therapists operating three independent radiation units, and two cancer surgeons. A third had died tragically of a malignant brain tumor, which killed him in seven weeks. The old doctor was long gone from the scene.

And what happened to the review of the accounts? The two senior surgeons fought us tooth and nail. For years! Finally, we learned that although many (six) of us had achieved partnership, our surgical colleagues were twice as equal as we were.

At the other end of my circuit, the oases of community health care were hungry for help and information. Physicians were tired of sending their patients to teaching centers and then hearing about their deaths months or years later, or not at all. The hospital nursing staffs were eager to learn about cancer care—they were bright, articulate, earnest, and hard working. Their recall of my discussions and instructions, and their genuine enthusiasm, was remarkable.

Over the next couple of years, I teamed with committed nursing supervisors to open areas, in several hospitals, dedicated to caring for patients with cancer.

Then, of course, came the patients and families themselves. That was what I was *supposed* to be all about, why I'd signed on in the first place. I was committed to the skills of evaluation and care I'd learned and honed while in training. That didn't change. It was time consuming and sometimes cumbersome. But when I set aside all the baloney about schedules, and driving, and selling my peculiar "image" of myself to referring physicians, it was my passion and my purpose. Over time, my commitment to supporting, comforting, and treating patients' cancers or their symptoms was as natural as breathing.

But there was another, new problem. My own need to mourn the deaths of most of my patients. There was no time for the luxury to retreat within myself, to convince myself that indeed I had done everything I could to delay an inevitable outcome.

It was a hard job for me. I could hold myself eternally responsible for each and all failures. That was still part of who I was. But that was time I spent squandering on myself while another patient knocked at the door. In time, I learned to draw a line I could not pass. To say, in effect, "I was honored to serve as your physician, caregiver, teacher, and friend. I treated you to prolong your life, or even to cure you. It's time that I must commit the same pledge to someone else now. I mourn. I will remember you and what you taught me."

It wasn't totally true. There have been untold, perhaps more than a thousand deaths. And now I cannot remember more than one or two faces. But I remember exactly how I felt each time. And I remember the last face.

CHAPTER SEVENTEEN

That was it. Pretty much my life during my first ten years in Southern California. I was tired. Back pain was a big problem. By the early 1980s I could not stand long enough to wait for an elevator. By day's end, I looked so miserable trudging from one room to the next that nurses looked on with sympathy and patients often moved over in their beds for me to either sit or lay next to them.

What had begun as a pain that came with prolonged standing, and had been my signal not to endure Baylor's aggressive surgical residency program, was now constant. I could tell when I brushed my teeth in the morning how bad the pain would be by midafternoon and after. I sought consultation from a noted orthopedist.

"There's nothing wrong with your back."

"Bullshit!"

I saw neurosurgeons and spine docs. Finally, in despair, I scoured the orthopedics' literature and found a case report of the first patient with spondylolisthesis. It was written in about 1880 and described a patient with exactly the same pain I had. The author called the anatomic disorder "spondylolisthesis." The vertebrae normally are stacked on top of one another like fat poker chips. They curve at the neck and just above the pelvis to help balance our top half on our bottom half. This poor fellow's lumbar spine (the five vertebrae between the ribs above and the pelvis below) was abnormal. The fifth, or lowest lumbar vertebra, had somehow moved from its stacked poker chip position and rested immediately *in front* of the spine below. This meant that the structures in front of the vertebrae, including the great artery and vein, and the spinal nerves, could have stretched or torn. They had, and he died, which is why pictures could be taken of his bones postmortem.

X-rays, which were not available to the poor guy, showed that I, too, had spondylolisthesis, only gratefully not as severe as the pioneer patient.

I was given narcotic pain medication, which relieved my pain but also made me high. I was able to work without pain, and I could do it around the clock. I scared myself! I was a snail with a brain without the pills, but I was flying a foot off the ground with them. It was not safe…what's more, everyone would *know* I had less pain—presumably from a drug.

I sought consultations from a respected neurosurgeon on the staff.

"Do you want the big operation or the little operation?"

"As little as I can get and still get better."

I underwent three major back operations over the next twelve months. The last one was the big operation: a fusion to immobilize my lower lumbar spine.

I was a monster at home during each convalescent period. After the first operation, I saw every movie—excluding pornography—in the local video store. After the second, I reread my basic medicine texts from cover to cover. After the third, I made five or six wooden model boats, often four feet high, rigged with billowing canvas sails. I had worked between the operations, and I had coverage of sorts, but I was sorely missed. In turn, I sorely missed the people in my charge.

They had become my friends. And more.

The dynamic I missed so much was treating patients. For example, of two pediatric cancer patients in my office, one was a beautiful towhead with sparkling blue eyes who had a tumor of his shoulder. The preferred treatment for him would have been removal of his upper limb and a radical dissection of the remaining tissues of his upper chest called a forequarter amputation. His mother refused. The likelihood of cure was low—he would ultimately die of his cancer. Under pressure, I agreed to treat him.

Two problems made him a huge challenge. The first was something called anticipatory nausea. Following each treatment performed in the hospital, he would begin to wretch and vomit at the mere sight of the place. So every three weeks for one and a half years, I would transport him to a different facility, start his IV myself, and administer his treatment. Then his mother would spend the night and offer her special support.

The second problem was more ominous. My nurses were women with small children. They were tortured by the kid's tribulations, particularly when he started to waste away. "Not another *child*—ever," they demanded.

Within a few months, we had another, an eight-year-old boy with cancer in his lymph nodes. We tried to say no politely and made extensive arrangements for him to be transferred to Children's Hospital in Los Angeles. But mother and child lay down in the office lobby and would not be moved. Exasperated, I called the referring physician.

"We need your help convincing this lady where the best care is."

"Sounds to me like she's made up her mind!"

We treated him. Years later, he graduated valedictorian of his high school class.

As my experience and reputation expanded, I took on panoply of positions at many of the hospitals I attended. One of my more fascinating adventures was to be selected as liaison between a community hospital and medical schools in Mexico and Central America. I traveled to many of them, was impressed by their curriculi, and worked to optimize their graduates' experience in the United States at several of my hospitals.

When chief of medicine at St. Vincent Medical Center, I was asked to supervise each admission of a doctor who was exclusively treating AIDS patients. This was the early days of the AIDS epidemic, and there were few therapeutic options and little clinical understanding of the disease. I could never forget what I learned there. I treated dozens of men with Kapsi's sarcoma, a tumor of skin which could spread like a prairie fire among those with terrible immune suppression. Pneumocysitis pneumonia had been a rarity, found only in immunosuppressed patients with lymphoma. Now it was epidemic!

During this entire period, down deep I cared not a fig for what I was being paid. I was made a full partner after my six and a half years, although I often wondered if my efforts were lost upon my senior partners. Our needs were more than generously met. My girls were happy. We had a level of comfort we'd never known before.

But I was still dogged by pain in the backs of my legs. After my third surgery, I determined to get a celebratory car. I'd been driving a Mazda RX-7, a two-seat, zippy little thing. But I was tired of this cursed pain, and I wanted something *more* as reward for my grit. I test-drove everything from Porsches to Ferraris. They were all too painful to sit in. Finally, I was approached by one of my office managers: her husband turbocharged Corvettes. Why not improve the performance of my little car?

Before I was through, I had installed custom seats, oversized brakes, and a racing suspension on that little beast. It couldn't be driven to its maximum performance anywhere but on a racecourse, and I had no stomach for that. But trips up and down the San Gabriel Mountains were spectacular.

Sara took it to a local party, had a beer, and drove it under the back end of a parked SUV. It was death for Walter Mitty! (Martha, now Elisabeth, backed the kids' Jeep into a tree. Every kid had to have one such experience, I guess.)

Anne's work as executive director of the Wellness Community Foothills was a paradigm shift for her. The organization was designed to provide free supportive care to cancer patients and their families. It was a need she well understood; she had listened to my expressions of frustration and helplessness for many years. Her steely spine shone like a beacon when truth as she knew it was clouded by politics or personality, and she relied on a consummate understanding of fact and purpose to guide her. I was overwhelmed—again--by my incredible good fortune that I had danced with the girl in the red dress.

After a couple of years in our starter home, we were able to put in a swimming pool. After my daughters screamed bloody murder for privacy, we added a second story to the house.

Three family events occurred at about that time. One was godsent. The others were sent by someone else.

The godsent one was a harbinger of sorts. I received a call from a researcher at Johns Hopkins. He was studying familial Alzheimer's disease, and would I come to Baltimore for evaluation? No way! I was approaching fifty and had two daughters. If I was to join my Nichamin forbears and exhibit rapid mental deterioration and death within five years, I would know it soon enough. And at such time, my wife and daughters would adjust accordingly. I had no intention of waiting for Damocles's sword to skewer me. Anne and the girls agreed.

What had happened to Esther? Leo put her into a nursing home, and fled to Montreal in the winter of 1973. There she survived for almost a decade, nourished by the fuel of her hatred.

Debbie was married now. And after the house on Homer Street was "empty", Debbie and her new husband backed a U-Haul truck against the garage and sacked the place, or so the tale is told.

In 1997 we received a call from the Kennedys in Montreal. Leo and his daughter-in-law, Patricia, were living and drinking together. And Pat was showing signs of liver failure. They had to be separated. No one else in the family could care for him.

Leo flew to LA; we received him on the tarmac. He was drunk. He had insisted on carrying his sword-cane onto the plane. It had been kept safe in the pilots' cabin and returned to him after the flight.

We tried to make Leo comfortable in our home. But he kept falling into the swimming pool at night. Our yellow Labrador, Maggie, saved his bacon on at least one occasion by dragging him to the shallow end of the pool.

We found an apartment near an area in Pasadena that featured used bookstores and quaint restaurants. He thrived there for a while, but his progressive loss of vision, caused by macular degeneration, made him morose and determined to end it all. If he couldn't read, he wouldn't live! Lacking weapons (except alcohol, which hadn't done the job—yet), he simply stopped eating.

I attended him on his last day. He had complained of severe abdominal pain. Examination demonstrated acute bowel obstruction, a condition that demanded abdominal surgery.

But Leo was ninety-three, and when I pulled the sheet covering him, I saw the starved body of a ten-year-old kid. His muscle mass was gone; his barrel chest looked absurd and ghoulish. He would never survive an operation. And what purpose would it serve? The nurses had given him a single Tylenol for his pain. He slept four hours. He complained of more pain. I had the nurses repeat the medication. Leo fell asleep and died.

During that period, Debbie and her husband had one son and adopted a daughter. Debbie protested that it was too difficult to drive from her home in Newton, Massachusetts, to Norwalk, so her mother was moved to a home in Boston. Anne visited on occasions when she traveled to Boston for Wellesley alumnae business.

On her last visit Anne was frightened by Esther's appearance. The old woman now resembled a waif and was curled into a fetal position. She was unresponsive. My wife called me.

"Do you think I should come there?" I asked.

"No! Don't come!" was Anne's imperative answer.

Esther died quietly thereafter.

In 2006, Debbie called me, scared to death. She needed help she was unable to find in Boston. She thought she had the family disease. More to the point, she needed help from the only family she still had. Her son had disappeared somewhere on the north shore of Hawaii's Big Island. His dream of commercialized, cookie-laden marijuana never happened. Her daughter Emily was married with children. She lived in New Hampshire. She was not reachable. We agreed to receive my sister and to find treatment for her. She arrived with a truckload of wardrobe boxes. When we opened the massive crates, we found a treasure trove of golden Tiffany knickknacks, sweaters, scarves, coats, shoes, and more. Few of them actually fit my sister. Most had never been worn.

She did not know where they'd come from. In short order, I received a call from a furious man calling from Boston. He had been in love with Debbie! But she had absconded with $30,000 he had put aside for their wedding. Deb had no clear memory of the man or the money.

My sister was then fifty-two years old. Phone discussions with friends and family revealed that my sister had demonstrated severe recent memory loss and strange behavior for the past two years. It was getting rapidly worse. After I obtained appropriate consultations, the work-up was completed and the diagnosis established—early-onset Alzheimer's disease. Debbie's expression of terror and horror was a sight I will never forget. It was mimicked exactly in her face some three years later, just before her death. It was a rigor, a death mask, as she arched her back grotesquely and strained against her leather restraints. I hear her piteous wails as I write this.

At the end, I refused to administer IV fluids to sustain her life. We scattered her ashes at sea. We returned the missing inventory to the jeweler's. The look of primal terror on her face just before she died haunts me nearly every night. I have never heard from her children.

My mother's pathology has continued to concern and confuse me. She clearly had Alzheimer's, because poor Debbie had it—and in its usual form.

But what about poor Esther's madness, her hatred, and her very slow deterioration? For years, and without any scientific proof, I believed that her hatred kept her alive, until even that part deep in her brain was destroyed, or at least isolated such that it could not perpetuate itself.

I came across part of the answer when reading a biography written about Leo by Ms. Patricia Morley. As his biographer, her major interest was about his life as a boy in England and his young adulthood as a budding artist in Montreal.

But as she described his infatuation with Esther's beauty, Pat mentioned that Esther had for years self-medicated with phenobarbital, and later with Miltown, the second-generation barbiturate that had been hailed as a nonaddictive therapy for stress and anxiety. (Like Valium and all the benzodiazepine class of drugs that have followed, the nonaddictive claim is false.) *That* was the huge stash of pills I had found as a youth! Esther had been protecting her drugs that day. I had forgotten all about the incident as I grew older, because mothers were never addicted to sedatives! And mine was so empty of warmth and affection but filled with hate for my father and...

Could drugs have done all of this?

Her addiction could explain other things as well. Like why she slept half the day long, why her eyes were glazed, why her mouth was dry, and why she made us wait three hours in the cold when it was her turn to pick us up from hockey practice. It could explain why she seemed withdrawn from and disinterested in all of us, except, of course, for her daughter.

More ominously, did her self-medication contribute to my prematurity, to my numerous congenital defects? It took me several years before I was brave enough to explore that issue and learn that, yes, it could have been so. How did I react to that knowledge? Stoically, I guess. Certainly, resentment and rage cannot repair the past.

But most unsettling of all, could her addiction to sedatives have contributed to her self-isolation in Minnesota, and could it have led to her hatred of my father for all the years I could remember—and its impact on our family? And could her drug-induced altered perceptions of perhaps *everything* have been causal to her bizarre attitude toward Debbie's failure frenzy?

Did her madness predate her Alzheimer's, or did one altered state simply merge with another?

For me, the most bizarre clinical observation at the end of her life was Esther's prolonged clinical course. For many years, I had been both resentful and anxious about whether my family was at risk for Alzheimer's. And now that time has answered that question, as a physician I wonder about consequence of two coexisting forms of mental illness.

I have not found answers to any of those questions. Nor have I really sought them. The fact that I, and my daughters, survived the family curse lets me off the hook a little bit in that regard. But I may someday again pursue that intersecting maze of unknowns.

While all that was occurring in my personal life, in the office, my policy was simple: we would see and care for anyone who walked through the door. If a patient wanted my help, I would discuss it with my staff, and we would offer it.

In the hospital, the same pledges held true. We had frequent meetings to discuss patients with medical or adjustment concerns. All members of the staff, from RN to LVN to nurse technician to transport personnel, were actively encouraged to give their input. If anyone objected to a plan, we'd review it, explain it again, and start over if needed. The quality of care, performance standards, and outcomes of the SVMC Oncology Unit—a 32-bed corner of a 265-bed hospital—became well known. Oncology was added to cardiac surgery, organ transplantation, and otology as signature specialties on the front face of the hospital.

CHAPTER EIGHTEEN

The next decades were witness to incredible changes in the business and the science of medical oncology practice in Los Angeles.

1. The change from an eight-hour to a twelve-hour shift for nursing personnel made it almost impossible to maintain the close-knit group of caregivers I had led in the past. Nurses worked for four days and then had three days to be with their families. But that extra day meant that they lost touch with the subtleties, and nuances, and even catastrophes that occurred to patients under their care. Often, nurses hired as temps from the nursing registry cared for our patients. Many were highly competent, but they understandably had no sense of the issues that had made the Oncology Unit caregivers so cohesive in their approach to their patients.

2. After harassing the hospital to provide our cancer patients and our staff with a therapist who could respond to their fears and uncertainties, I hired one myself; I paid him out of pocket for several years. He met with the nurses regularly and helped them air out their concerns and complaints. He was also available to consult with individual patients and families when needed.
3. "Alternative medicine" was becoming a buzzword in the lay press. Virtually all such therapy was based on testimonials rather than scientific, controlled trials. But it was hard to convince patients of the differences. So I invited an herbal specialist to occupy part of my office for free. I gave him the space and access to my patients. I praised his skills and advertised his presence to other physicians at SVMC. The man was a Jew from New York City. He'd spent several years in China learning acupuncture, herbal therapy, and other modalities of Chinese medicine. At a tumor board, I announced that he was available to any physician in the hospital who wished to use his services for their patients. My purpose was twofold. First, he could help with some forms of chemotherapy toxicity. Second, his approach might keep some patients (or, more usually, families) from demanding treatment like laetrile or eye of newt, and then running off to Mexico to die untreated by effective agents. It worked so well that the hospital soon gave him his own office and staff. He became a small profit center for them.

4. In the 1980s, not much emphasis was placed on wellness for cancer patients. Anne introduced me to two young men who were willing to offer their brand of exercise therapy to our patients at no cost to them. They met twice weekly. I supported their efforts for a year, and then the hospital began to pick up their tab. That program recently had its twenty-fifth anniversary.
5. In the early days of my practice, patients were frequently referred from outlying communities for treatment and supportive care. (I was still serving those areas too.) After I centered my practice in one location, those referrals began to disappear. But there were densely populated regions around the hospital that needed cancer care services. I felt it was imperative to expand our referral base in the most densely populated region of LA.--in our own back yard.

I adapted to the needs of the local communities, and delved into new areas of clinical research. I knew that liver cancer was a frequent, usually fatal cancer among Koreans, who populated a nearby community. No one had ever actually tried to screen for liver cancer, to define its presence early, and hopefully increase the chances for a cure. So I did it. I obtained a modest grant and then went to community doctors, churches, and gathering houses to present my pitch. A Korean community service organization supported our efforts actively. Alas, the study was negative—the cure rate was not improved—but it opened the door for a flood of physician applications to the medical staff. Later, the hospital opened an entire floor dedicated to care of Korean patients. The same sort of process was repeated as the hospital sought to attract Japanese doctors and their patients.

By the mid-1990s, my practice was so large that keeping records straight and lines of communication open to referring physicians became overly laborious. So I instituted an electronic medical record (EMR) system. Each patient's diagnosis, medications, other medical problems, allergies, cancer treatments, and toxicities were immediately available to the entire office staff. As had been my practice, any one of them could red flag something that seemed wrong. Prepared notes to referring doctors were sent by fax or snail mail. Twenty years later, the EMR was becoming the expected standard of inter-office communication.

In order to protect our patients (and ourselves) from errors in administration of chemotherapy drugs, we turned early on to a special storage and documentation system for our chemotherapy agents. Fifteen years later, it has become a standard of care among all oncologists' offices and chemotherapy treatment centers. We were among the first to implement it in Southern California. Before administering a drug, the nurse had to double-check my written order with previous orders documented in the system. Then she would remove the desired drug from the storage unit, cross-check its identification with another nurse, remove the desired dosage, document it in the system, and check it again with a colleague before administering the drug.

During all the years of its use, we had only a single error. A newly hired chemotherapy nurse, with good tickets from an outstanding institution, gave a lethal dose of chemo to a patient. She had picked up the wrong bottle from the rack, had assumed it was the desired drug, and had proceeded through the entire double-check process. The patient's death, weeks later, caused a terrible ache in all our hearts. . It was a trauma that none of us forgot.

I saw several Philippine nurses every year. Invariably they were in their fifties or early sixties. They conveyed a sense of passive defeat and impending doom in their speech and general demeanor. When I performed a physical exam, I found a breast that had been totally replaced by tumor Enlarged, rock hard lymph nodes, some of them draining clear, yellowish fluid, marched up the chest wall and into the axilla--the drainage meant dead (necrotic) tumor. The cancer deposits had outgrown their own blood supply over time and had died. The odor from necrotic tissue was unmistakable, unforgettable. How had these women been able to tolerate the pain of tumor invading the ribs below their breast? How had they covered the smell, when they were with friends or family? Or when they were alone? How had they dealt with their terror as they watched their bodies being slowly destroyed?

These were trained medical personnel who had first isolated themselves, then ignored the truth of their disease, and finally accepted the inevitability of a terrible, painful death. Had they ever, ever had a breast exam? Why not? This cancer, if identified ten--or even fifteen--years ago, had been curable!!

This could not happen again! I conceived yet another project. With a small grant from the Daughters of Charity

Foundation, we forayed again into the community. I gave talks all over Philippine Town about the need for early diagnosis of breast cancer, and identified the facilities where they could be obtained, often at reduced cost. But in addition, I asked that audience members complete a questionnaire. In sum, it asked, "Do you undergo routine mammography? Does your doctor examine your breasts regularly?" The answers were nearly unanimous.

"My doctor never told me to go."

The problem lay with the general practitioners themselves. But was it a cultural taboo? I couldn't know until I asked.

I traveled to the lion's den. I invited about thirty primary care doctors from the area within a mile or two of SVMC. These were busy physicians with large outpatient practices (the population density in the area was perhaps the highest in Los Angeles). They rarely admitted patients to a hospital, and generally did not participate in professional education updates at nearby medical centers.

I presented our findings, and asked, "What's the deal? Women in your community are dying from advanced breast cancer. Unnecessarily! Here are the data. Screening works! It saves lives! Is it a societal taboo to touch a patient's breast? We can help with that. We can get out the word. Ladies may flock to you for exams and scheduled X-rays."

The responses were pretty noncommittal. In following weeks showed no change in referrals to the mammography center. I contacted the leader of the group and got an "I'm trying as hard as I can" response.

So we addressed the women themselves. I talked to community centers, church groups, and home gatherings.

I provided free breast examinations in my office. We arranged for reduced cost mammography, and offered free transportation when it was needed.

Somehow, I struck a nerve with both the women and the Daughters of Charity.

The Daughters allowed me to hire a bright, outgoing young Philippine man who took over the task of encouraging women to go to my office for free breast exams, and to the radiographic facility for mammography. He recruited others to examine women's breasts as part of a free screening program. His work continues to this day as part of the hospital's community outreach program.

As more years passed, I became more involved in political and strategic issues at St. Vincent Medical Center. I had served as the Medicine Department chair in the mid-1980s and had been chief of staff at a smaller hospital in East Los Angeles.

I'd had my fill of responsibilities that took me away from teaching and patient care. But in 2007, I was approached by two old and dear friends who coaxed me into declaring myself a candidate for the elected position as president of the medical staff at St. Vincent Hospital.

I had not the slightest inkling of the next catastrophic change awaiting me just down the road—literally.

CHAPTER NINETEEN

In less than a second, it was over.
On October 10, 2008, I was driving along a residential street a mile from home. In less time than it took to say WTF, I lost consciousness. My car veered to the left and up a gently sloping ancient Chinese rock wall about three feet in width.

When I awoke, my vehicle was on its top, with me suspended from my seat belt. I scrambled loose and kicked my way through a side window. I stood alone on Virginia Road, embarrassed and confused, but uninjured, I thought. The local police arrived while I called Anne to relate what little I knew.

I was taken to the local hospital ER. The examining physician pronounced me clinically okay, but I underwent a CAT scan of the brain to make sure there had been no bleeding. An EEG showed a seizure focus—a potential cause of my sudden loss of consciousness. I was examined by a neurologist, who gave me a medication to suppress any future seizure. I was shaken, but not nearly as much as my family, it seemed. They were really worried.

I returned to work the next day. I had patients to see and a lecture to give.

And the next day and the next. But six days after the accident, I began experiencing severe pain in the back of my head and neck. I passed out in our kitchen...

I was taken to the ER again--with sirens and flashing lights, again. A repeat CAT scan now showed that there was blood between the leathery outer covering of my brain, the dura mater, and the brain itself. Enough blood had accumulated that the brain stem, the upmost extension of the spinal cord and the center for most reflex activity—like breathing—was being pushed through the opening at the base of my skull, the foramen magnum. The brain was spongy and compressible. Blood was not. It was one of those medically rare, genuine emergencies. Unless the blood was evacuated from my subdural space in a *real* hurry, I was toast.

I was rushed to the operating room. The neurosurgeon chiseled a hole in one side of my skull. Blood spurted everywhere. But my brain was decompressed.

And that, I would like to say, was that!

Not so. A follow-up scan demonstrated continued bleeding at several other sites inside my noggin. Over the next week or so, I was operated on five more times before the bleeding was controlled. One of the surgeries had involved placing a tube into the water-containing cavity at the center of my brain (ventricle) to prevent excess pressure on my compressible brain cells by removing uncompressible fluid (blood or spinal fluid) when needed. Sort of like adding brake fluid to a car, but in reverse.

Here, I must insert three postulates of medical practice, based solely on my experience as doctor and patient:

1. Doctors are not only the worst patients—they often have the most complex problems.
2. Kennedy's law (so designated by me) of reoperation states that if the mortality rate of a given surgery is, say, 1 percent, it goes up a bit, perhaps even doubles, if the procedure must be repeated.
3. With any successive operations, the infection risk and the mortality rate begin to soar. By the sixth surgery, infection is a virtual certainty.

And sure enough, I got mine. *Serratia marcesens* was its name. My wife first noted it as she came to visit one Saturday. Her steel trap mind recalled the effluvia I occasionally wore home from the ER. With an extremely sophisticated nose in her own right, Anne smelled pus when the elevator doors opened on my floor. It got stronger—and fouler—as she walked toward the ICU—and my bed.

Still following her nose, she lifted one of my bandages and saw the source of the smell. As she told me later, thick, fetid pus was draining around the tube at the base of my skull. The organism was identified as *Serratia marcesens*. I spent the next two months in ICU receiving huge doses of intravenous antibiotics. My only memory of that period was that my hair and my skull were constantly on fire. And the pain went on for hours, and days, and forever.

As the torture continued, I requested a conference with the infectious disease consultant.

"Let me die. Please. Just let me go."

"I can't do that. You've been very sick for a long time. But you're getting better now."

Better enough to what?

Anne never knew about that discussion.

When I left the ICU, I could not speak. I could not stand. I had almost constant, uncontrollable diarrhea. I had lost forty pounds, despite being offered three squares a day. My fundamental problem was that I couldn't figure out how to order my meals or how to get them to my mouth when they arrived.

Before I was hospitalized, my feet were like anybody else's. When I left, they were constantly cold and burning. Later, an experienced and trusted neurologist identified the cause.

"I think it's POW neuropathy, the peripheral nerve damage suffered by some prisoners of war. It's due to prolonged malnutrition. As you know, it is progressive. There is ongoing damage to sensation, position sense, and motor strength."

As I write this page, my nerve conduction tests have deteriorated an additional 25 percent over the past two years compared to my original measurements. Sometimes, I can feel the numbness and the pain creeping s-l-o-w-l-y up my legs. I cannot think of anyone I dislike personally enough to wish this malady upon.

Rehabilitation was intensive. And I did improve, first in mental acuity, then speech, and then in physical strength. After many months of speech therapy and physical strengthening, I tried to return to my patients and to my job as president of the medical staff at St. Vincent Medical Center.

But for the first time in my adult life, I *was a failure!*. I couldn't work harder, or longer, or think faster as I'd done since before I could remember. I had always been driven --first to survive and later to excel.

But now, I couldn't keep up. I saw but few outpatients from my practice. My patients welcomed me with hugs and loving words. Then they were directed to see another physician in my group. Those patients assigned to me were considered malcontents—they demanded to see me and no one else, even after my long absence. I soon learned that the basis of their complaints was the inadequate time they were given to understand their disease process and its treatment.

It was my office. The waiting room was filled with my patients, many of them longtime cancer survivors. But things were different. I felt dated as a dinosaur. My treatment style had made me an anachronism…and perhaps less.

During my recovery, I had sold my practice to an old and trusted friend who had himself been forced to retire because of a neurological disorder. Our practices were a good fit, and my patients had to have continuity of care, delivered as they had come to know and expect. I had actually approached his group before the accident and presented my case. Anne and Liz had completed the negotiations while I was still was struggling to survive an infection that had an 80 percent mortality rate. The numbers said I was cooked. But my patients needed care with or without me.

As I prepared to see my patients, I became aware that my appearance was downright scary. I was cue-ball bald. I had scars from craniotomies. When my hair began to regrow, I had a hairless stripe from my hairline to the back of my skull, as if I'd been scalped. (It was skin grafted from my thigh to cover an infected section of my skull, which could not otherwise heal.) I had scars from the plastic plugs put into my skull to cover the holes. Without them I would have had multiple fontanels, like a baby—but they would never close. I'd be easy prey for any six-year-old with a sharp pencil.

As for my ability as physician and leader of my medical staff, my brain was five words behind the words that came out of people's mouths. Where I once had reveled in keeping ten balls in the air at any given instant, now I couldn't manage holding one! And the fatigue was awful! Walking from the parking lot to my office was more than I could bear. I was given a medicine once used to keep soldiers in Afghanistan awake and alert. It helped a bit, but by midafternoon, I was physically and mentally exhausted anyway. There was just nothing left of me.

Anne was scared to let me drive. She was right. Even after short trips to the store, I couldn't find my way home. We hired a college kid to drive me to and from meetings and clinics.

As for the much-heralded president-of-staff position, I failed at that too. I struggled to fulfill my duties and to serve as mentor and rallying point for the several hundred doctors on the staff who were even now facing huge changes in the way they practiced their craft. There were moments when my experience of four decades and my logical approach to defining problems and exploring essential variables—and listening to others' perspectives—just appeared. And those moments were wonderful. But mostly I was too exhausted, and handicapped by the damage done to my nervous system, to be on top of multiple ongoing crises. I had a tremor in my left hand, and the fingers themselves were weak. On one occasion I joined other doctors at lunch. I couldn't get a soup spoon to my mouth with any soup in it! I felt the uneasy looks I got from men I'd known for years. I gave up trying to eat and listened in silence.

I approached the hospital CEO and admitted, "I can't do this!"

I called a meeting of the general medical staff. Loyal colleagues, and those who were simply curious, packed the meeting hall. I expressed gratitude for their confidence.

"I love many of you like brothers or sisters. We have fought wars together as comrades *and* antagonists, and delighted in our victories. I am humbled by the trust you've placed in me. I recognize how tenuous the times are for you and me. But I can't do what you've elected me to do, or represent your interests optimally. I simply cannot do this well enough."

My speech was slow and faltering. It took a patient listener to hear what I had to say. I was done.

Following my discharge from ICU, I was also plagued by diarrhea for more than 5 years, due to intestinal infestation with a nasty bacterium called *Clostridium difficile.* The bacterium characteristically appears in patients who receive long courses of antibiotics. That was me! I desperately lacked energy, and I felt sick and weak all the time. I was treated and re-treated for this infection, sometimes for a year at a time. I had second and third opinions. I was colonoscoped and cultured time and time again. Even when the bug was not identified, I *knew* when it was there.

Finally, my gastroenterologist suggested that I would have this condition for good, with occasional relapses.

"That's bullshit! I will not accept that!"

In frustration, anger, and despair, I finally said, "To hell with standard medical practice!" and I underwent a Fecal Microbial Transfer (FMT), or, colloquially, a poop transplant. The surgeon who performed the procedure indicated that the poop donor be someone who ate the same foods and had the same environmental exposures as me.

"That's got to be either Anne or Mollie the Wonder Dog."

"No dogs. Not yet, anyway."

The following morning, Anne donated her fecal bacteria, which were delivered into my large bowel through a colonoscope, as a diluted, liquefied solution, which was sprayed over the surface of my colon.

The trip home—across town amid commuter traffic—was leaky and uncomfortable for both Anne and me. But by the very next day, I was stronger. I was able to act a little more like the *me* I remembered.

Six months after the procedure, I felt pretty normal, with one major exception.

My chronic back pain, which I came to live with and to adapt to, was now awful. I took physical therapy and worked with a personal trainer for over two years.

In the early spring of 2014, I began to lose strength in my legs. Anne felt it was due to my lack of exercise, but to me, the weakness was the reason I could not exercise as I had. I went from daily two-mile walks with Mollie to a trudge around the block once or twice a week. Then not at all. Increasingly, my posture was bent over like a broken soda straw or a little old man.

In addition, I was having more trouble with urination. Was it an old man's big prostate, or nerve damage?

I sought help from a variety of consultants. Ultimately, I underwent my fourth back surgery to release my trapped nerve roots. A rind of scar tissue was squeezing the roots as they traveled just below the lower end of the spinal cord. The operation was successful, but postoperatively, the surgeon advised me that it would take a year or more for my back and my spinal nerves to recover.

To me it was, is, and will be an impossible eternity. Patience has never been my strong suit. But what choice do I have?

CHAPTER TWENTY

I did not take this series of traumatic events, and their consequences, with courage or grace. From before I could remember, I had wanted to be a physician. I had worked long and hard to build an office, gather a loyal staff of loyal, highly competent assistants, develop a business which provided a living for my wife and me, and serve a cadre of colleagues who respected and depended on me even as they learned about the disease afflicting their patient. I had been recognized for my work in basic science and clinical research. I had received special recognition from *U.S. News & World Report* for the caliber and consistency of my work.

Now I was empty, alone, and without value to others.

What was I to do? During the first six months after the accident, I frequently considered killing myself, something I could not discuss with Anne or the kids. I was too weak, and in too much pain. My past was done. I could see no future. But I had a terrible, sometimes almost tangible *need* to contribute something, somehow. My brain was scarred, but it wasn't dead. I had more to give—somehow.

Finally, a thought occurred, although it scared the hell out of me. When I was growing up, despite the dysfunctions in our family, I loved, and perhaps revered, my father's skill as a writer.

Where did that stuff *come from*? I could *never* produce that in a million years!

His single piece of word-craft advice to me rang loudly in my head.

"Write about what you know."

I considered my options. I was not going to die today or tomorrow. My legacy was no longer my achievements or my explorations in medicine or in medical research. I had recently fought battles for survival and recovery that my colleagues and patients could not ever understand. No more did I want to play catch up to internalize the bevy of new modalities of cancer treatment that had been introduced during my illness.

As time passed, I realized that whatever my contributions to medicine had been, they would be quickly forgotten—or never even recognized--by younger physicians who followed me. The only people who would remember me were the patients I cured, or those whose lives had been prolonged, and perhaps the families whom I helped along the way. Most important, I realized that my greatest contribution to patients, families, and medical staffs alike had been my willingness to listen well, and then to advise as honestly as I could, based on the information at hand.

That had required patience, and time. But time was a luxury that few physicians had in 2015. I watched with alarm as the doctor who had replaced me now saw twelve patients in an hour—five minutes per cancer patient! I simply could not do that...*ever.* And he was following that schedule not out of preference, but simply to cover the overhead of his practice!

I realized I was truly a dinosaur, too tired, too old, and too scarred to joust against this new flood tide, which will irrevocably change medical care in the future.

Instead, I determined to write about my experiences during the happiest, most challenging times of my life. I bought a zillion books on how to write; I actually read a few. The sanest instructions were consistent: just sit down and begin to write.

But even today, more than six years after I saw my last cancer patient, I carry a persistent ache for that last one. He was a middle-aged businessman. But he was elegant. He was tall and lean, and dark as ebony. He moved with such grace! He had been a medal winner in a past Olympics. But now he had a metastatic nasopharyngeal cancer, an extremely difficult tumor to treat. I managed to induce a remission and keep him fully functional for many months with chemotherapy. But then the tumor showed itself again in his long bones, where it caused terrible pain. Despite this, he walked and funtioned normally for a while. But after two successive hospital admissions, one for treatment of an abnormally high blood calcium level, and a second for pain management he rejected further therapy and opted to die at home. I visited with him, his wife, and their adult son frequently before his death. The fact that I could not do anything more to help him has eaten at my heart as painfully as it had with the very first patient I treated—and lost--decades before. I never knew why I hurt so badly for that man. He was the last among countless patients who died under my care.

It is amply rewarding that my legacy will be my long-loving, infinitely wise wife, whom I still adore, and whose grit and steely spine I had never recognized in our early days together. It is in my daughters, their husbands, and their children, who for better or worse carry much of Anne and me in their DNA.

And today, that is enough, perhaps, for any man.

So why do I write this inexact collection of experiences and memories? Because that is part of *my* hard wiring--after all.

ACKNOWLEDGEMENTS

I owe my father, John Leo Kennedy, a debt I cannot repay. As a boy, I was entranced by my perception of Leo Kennedy, 'the writer'. Later, I envied his friends; their easy wit, their camaraderie, their secret society. But I knew I could never create the things he had produced.

There were great gaps in what I understood about him. Most glaring was his skill and imagination, things that he could not teach me, because he couldn't describe their origin or expression himself. I hid from that perceived deficiency in me, sought other paths and was much rewarded in countless ways. Only when I had no choice, no other place to hide, did I try my hand at storytelling.

My wife, Anne has helped me immensely in this effort. She knows every pore of my skin, and has somehow learned to sleep beside the quiet click-click of my mechanical heart valve. Anne has literally saved my life more than once. And now she's done it again.

Most recently, she dragged me back from a pit of self-pity, where it seemed that every time I found a hand-hold to pull myself out, the walls collapsed in on me again.

She demanded that I try to write. She made me get off my butt and attend a class on creative writing. Then, when I doubted that I could prompt someone to laugh, or sigh, or weep, or even to be entertained, she slapped me around a little herself.

"You're like Leo. You embellish. You play tricks. You dart in and out of the truth! You tell good stories. Just DO it! And see what happens."

I'm grateful to the late Al Martinez, the Bard of Los Angeles, and a much-respected, long time columnist for the L.A. Times. It was his course I attended. He put up with my lip, enjoyed my word craft, and when he received my first effort at a short story, said, "Now write the damn book!"

So I did.

Al died before I finished this piece, and left me no blueprint about what to do next. I've been a physician for 5 decades. Complete a book, or save a life…give me a medical crisis anytime. I was paralyzed by the prospect of navigating the boiling seas of the publishing trade in my wood-framed, hide-covered little boat, without no star to guide me.

Enter Nancy Fulton, a Los Angeles writer, producer and teacher who heard my cries for help on the Internet. Within minutes of our first email exchange, she had pointed me in the proper direction, and did all the heavy lifting, which has got us here. Her patience, and remarkable expertise, is without doubt the reason you're reading this today.

More important, she's become a friend, a colleague, a mentor and more. She's the reason you've (hopefully) enjoyed this book. Without Nancy's expertise, I'd still be walking in tight little circles, going nowhere. Blessings to you, my friend.

Peter Kennedy, M.S., M.D.
August, 2015

Made in the USA
Lexington, KY
25 October 2015